THE

POWER

OF

APOLOGY

JAMES TAWIAH MENSAH

Published by GloriPub
©Copyright 2018 James Tawiah Mensah
Unless otherwise stated, all Scripture quotations are taken from the
Holy Bible, New International Version (NIV) Full Life Study Bible.
Copyright 1985, 1995, 2002 by Zondervan Publishing House.
ISBN-10: 0997621303
ISBN-13: 9780997621303

Also by James Tawiah Mensah

SUCCESS: WHAT IS IT ALL ABOUT?

GIVING: WHAT IS IT ALL ABOUT?

LOYALTY: WHAT IS IT ALL ABOUT?

THE WORD OF GOD vs. THE WORK OF GOD

THE LAST COAT: JOSEPH'S JOURNEY TO THE
PALACE

TO GOD BE THE GLORY

Contents

Acknowledgement

My late parents, Mr. Abednego Aklama Mensah and Mad. Christiana Charkuor Charway, whose words of wisdom and character shaped mine; Nii Omensu IV (aka Ebenezer Oblebu Mensah, the Asafoatse, Naazen We of Prampram); my brothers, Rev. Michael Martey Mensah, Ghana and Nigeria; Mr. James Martey Mensah, Mr. William Mensah and sisters; late Ms. Adelaide Adoley Mensah, Ms. Belinda Marteykuor Mensah, Ms. Ruth Akweley Mensah, Ms. Letitia Agoyo Mensah and Ms. Alberta Abah Mensah, all in Ghana, whose contributions, in various times and ways, also helped to make me what I am today.

Rev. Benjamin Kwadjo Boakye, Senior Pastor, Ebenezer Assembly of God Church, Bronx, New York, USA, my present pastor, made me the

Superintendent, Sunday School Department, and provided the tools needed to succeed. Rev. Emmanuel Yawson. My good buddies, Brother George Kwame Arkhurst and Minister Tony Aghamiogie and fellow Sunday School teachers, encouraged me in diverse ways.

Also, the students who listen to me every Sunday inspired me with their contributions in class. All Department leaders and entire members of Ebenezer Assembly of God Church, Bronx, New York, USA, gave me the opportunity to use my talent and gift to serve; Mr. Awuku Darko, Armor-bearer, Living Faith Ministry Int., Mount Vernon, New York, USA, and his wife, Sister Unity Agyeman, stood by me during the writing with words of encouragement. Mr. and Mrs. Isaac and Judith Amoah, Bronx, New York, USA; Mr. and Mrs. Raymond and Abigail Kotei, West Haven, Connecticut, USA, my biggest fans; Mr. Joseph Nartey, my brother-in-law, Bronx, New York, USA; a very, very good friend, Pastor Isaac Twumasi, Ghana; Mr. Patrick Lucas Onasis Aryerh, Ghana, (aka P.L.O Aryerh); Mrs. Anna Christa Rawls Sackey, edited and wrote the foreword for "Success: What is it all about?" Rev. William Kanych, Senior

Pastor, Faith Assembly of God, Yonkers, New York, USA, edited and wrote the foreword for "Giving: What is it all about?" Rev. Nancy Pierre, edited and wrote the foreword for "Loyalty: What is it all about?" Pastor Kwame Acheampong, author, "Fashion and Faith," and Ms. Joyce Ohene-Amoah, author, "Building A Healthy Lasting Marriage," inspired me.

Reviews

"Minister James Mensah's books are so captivating. When you start, you can't put them down. His intricating way of weaving the biblical stories together makes him extraordinary - you need to get these books."

Mrs. Patricia Abboah.

Introduction

"If your brother or sister sins, go and point out their fault, just between the two of you. If they listen to you, you have won them over. But if they will not listen, take one or two others along, so that 'every matter may be established by the testimony of two or three witnesses.' If they still refuse to listen, tell it to the church; and if they refuse to listen even to the church, treat them as you would a pagan or a tax collector." (Matthew 18 :15-17)

"Apology is not a bullet, yet so powerful enough to penetrate the steel walls of unforgiveness." (Author)

She sat all by herself. With her arms folded across her chest, the aura of stillness and silence emanating from her isolation spoke loudly. I was convinced she was not aware of the signal she was sending out. Her eyes were fixated on her pastor, who was preaching with this charismatic prowess from behind the pulpit. She sat quietly. To say the least, that was her posture throughout the service, ever since I entered the sanctuary that cold afternoon. But this kind of posture, which I had never witnessed before, curiously captured my attention. I was awe-stricken by her demeanor. Something had gone wrong. And I sensed it confidently. "What is it? I cannot imagine her being so quiet on a given Sunday," I thought of it. The 'Amens,' the 'Praise the Lord's' and the 'Hallelujah's,' this woman was known for, were missing. It was too surreal. That was unlike her. This is not the lady I knew over the years. Then my impulse kicked in to know the reason behind this demeanor. From then onwards, I couldn't be as attentive as I would have loved to be to hear the word of God. Yes, I couldn't focus on the message. So, I turned intermittently to look at her direction as the preaching went on. Every time I looked she sat quietly. And I pitied her. Therefore, immediately the service ended, I dashed to find out what exactly was going on with her. To my surprise, my worst fears were ascertained. Something was indeed worrying my friend. It'd taken absolute control over her. It left her a bundle of sorrows and disturbances though a powerful message was coming from the pulpit.

Nancy (pseudonym) and I became friends through her pastor. Nancy's pastor requested for some pieces of information on a pressing issue from my pastor. Those pieces of information were in my custody then. We had to meet as a result, so this request could be satisfied. In the course of dispensing this information, I interacted with her numerous times. Nancy, who was deeply involved during those interactions, became an acquaintance. This unplanned and twisted relationship gave me the opportunity to visit them whenever the chance presented itself. I was therefore a familiar face to the whole church. It was on one such visit that I was confronted with this whole experience. When I realized that things were not in harmony I became disturbed.

Nancy's eyes were moistened and red. I noticed it as soon as I stood by her. It was not normal for her to be found in such state. I could easily assume she had been crying. I never hesitated to express my shock, which manifested in the series of questions I piled on her.

"What is going on with all these tears and red eyes?" I inquisitively queried. Without waiting for an answer, I volleyed another one across to her.

"And why are you so isolated and quiet during a Sunday service?"

"Nothing." Nancy shot back passively, as if my questions were not relevant; as if to deter me from digging further for the reasons.

"Really? Are you sure?" I probed further. I was not convinced enough by her response. So, I pushed back again with all my energy.

I forcefully countered her response, saying, "Nancy, you're trying to run away from your own shadow. You cannot do that. It's not possible. It's all over you that something is not well. It won't do you any good if you tried to remain stuck in your shells. It would be better if you would come out of this shell you created for yourself. In fact, it would be the best if you laid everything on the table, so we can talk about them."

Nancy was touched so she jerked. Then she cleared her throat. I assumed she was ready to discuss the issues. Not at all. I was tricked by that gesture. She was still hesitant. By this time, I sat down and pulled the chair toward her. Looking straight into those disappointed eyes, I made the final appeal to her conscience.

"You are a Christian, and for God's sake, not just a mere Christian, but a matured one, Nancy," I said, "and therefore, cannot be walking with tons of load on your chest if you've been wronged. I think you have to voice out the issues." And she cracked. She opened herself up and narrated her version of what is it that was 'choking' her.

"Someone offended me a few days ago," she started slowly without any attempt to look at me in the eyes. "And to tell you truth, I am really hurt," she said. "I have been praying over it ever since so God will take the pain out of me, but to no avail."

I sat there baffled by her convictions regarding solution to offences that might have been committed against a Christian. I hesitated a little bit to comment on her beliefs, but I mustered the courage and responded.

Interjecting, I asked, "Is this the reason you look so different today?"

She answered, affirming my assumption, but reluctantly. Then I asked if she had approached the person with her concerns; the offence the person committed against her.

"No, I have not relayed my concerns to the person," she answered faithfully.

Without making any attempt to condemn her, I said, "This is not what the Bible says about the way we should solve problems when we are wronged. In fact, Jesus vividly outlined how we should sort issues out with our neighbors if we were offended."

I did not waste time at all. Then I quoted the scriptures where Jesus plainly said;

> If your brother or sister sins, go and point out their fault, just between the two of you. If they listen to you, you have won them over. But if they will not listen, take one or two others along, so that 'every matter may be established by the testimony of two or three witnesses.' If they still refuse to listen, tell it to the church; and if they refuse to listen even to

the church, treat them as you would a pagan or a tax collector. (Matthew 18 :15-17)

Looking at her face I suspected she was surprised by the quote I used to oppose her stand. I believed she had not given any consideration to her understanding of that scripture. I continued and said,

"My dear, it is never said anywhere in the Bible that we pray over an offence committed against us for God to solve it amicably and take the hurt away."

"This had been the message preached from the pulpit over the years. Sorry to say it is wrong to go about it in that manner. I will suggest you approach the person, present the way you felt, and are feeling even now, so you can trash out the whole issue," I counselled her.

After these few minutes of conversation with Nancy, I excused myself to see her pastor. I had a short discussion with him. When I finished chatting with him, I asked for permission to leave. Seeing that she was still glued to her chair, I waved her good-bye, promising to be in touch soon.

This is not an isolated case. It is not typical only to Nancy, but to many Christians populating the pews in our churches. Many are going through similar experiences. They don't know what to do. They lack the knowledge. They had prayed without approaching the offender. This is what we have been taught over the years. We think, by so doing we are obeying the command of God and therefore will be in good standing with Him. No, not at all.

Because the message of forgiveness had frequented and flooded our pulpits, whatever the case might be, we are inclined to immediately begin the process of forgiveness. We have been deluged with these messages for a longtime, spanning years. And we've bought into it ignorantly. Apology had no place in these pulpits because no one had ever made any attempt to use it as part of settling a dispute. In their book, *"The Five Languages of Apology,"* the authors said this of the usual Christian approach to problems. I quote,

> Some, particularly within the Christian worldview, have taught forgiveness without apology. They often quote the words of Jesus, 'If you do not forgive men their trespasses, neither will your Father forgive your

trespasses.' Thus, they say to the wife whose husband has been unfaithful and continues in his adulterous affairs, "You must forgive him, or God will not forgive you." Such an interpretation of Jesus' teachings fails to reckon with the rest of the scriptural teachings on forgiveness. (Chapman G. and Thomas J., 2006)

Apology is not part of our Christian narratives when it comes to settling issues between two feuding folks or factions. It seemed to have been lost in our biblical worldview. Rarely is it mentioned to the offender. Instead, the offended - reeling under pain from the offence - is coerced, pushed and even condemned, to forgive. Immediately after, as a way of advising or encouraging the offended, it would be followed by the usual quote that "... *if you do not forgive others their sins, your Father will not forgive your sins*" (Matthew 6:15). The offended would yield but reluctantly thereby leaving the relationship still fractured.

For the sake of its importance in our Christian journey, I will implore you to join me to consider, at least, these very serious instances in the Bible where apology played vital roles. It was the expression of apology that compelled the offended to accept the olive branches extended by the offenders, making the whole scenario worthy of emulation. This will enable us to properly appreciate its role in finding solutions to problems we will encounter among us.

James Tawiah Mensah

Chapter 1

MY LORD
Jacob and Esau

"He instructed the one in the lead: "When my brother Esau meets you and asks, 'Who do you belong to, and where are you going, and who owns all these animals in front of you?' then you are to say, 'They belong to your servant Jacob. They are a gift sent to my lord Esau, and he is coming behind us.'" He also instructed the second, the third and all the others who followed the herds: "You are to say the same thing to Esau when you meet him." (Genesis 32:17-19)

"Apology is that lubricant that lubricates the turning wheels of forgiveness. Its absence will cause the wheels to twist and turn, making the journey unpleasant." (Author)

1

The riveting story between these two brothers had frequently captured many a pulpit over the past years. In fact, if the number of its appearances at these pulpits could be tallied, it would have run into millions. Emotional messages were preached from it and forgiveness examples were derived as means to settle issues. This is a story when narrated, touches nerves and makes lives move to a seat's edge. It is touted as one of the strong examples to cite when the subject of forgiveness is raised. The tactics Jacob used to claim what belonged to Esau was absurd and disgusting. The tactics were so ridiculous and uninspiring it should have no place in any society. These cheating and deceptive attitudes toward his elder brother should be described as wicked and senseless. It's a daylight robbery against a sibling and must be condemned in no uncertain terms. Yes, it deserves such attributes of condemnation. But, at the same time, it's the intensity of Jacob's plots that gave this forgiveness narrative a flavor. It is the magnitude of his deceptions that creates emotions when the story is told; that despite all that happened, his elder brother brushed them aside and boldly embraced him. In all these circumstances that ensued, there was one ingredient that had been over looked all along. No one had ever mentioned it. Had it been absent in their meeting, it would have made Esau jittery and the story might have ended differently. What was it that made Esau to have easily forgiven his younger brother for these atrocities he committed against him? What was it that moved his heart to act in this manner? We will attempt to unearth that factor.

Offence Committed

It was a sacred moment they had allotted themselves, so they can commune with the LORD. It was a time they set aside to pray. A time they privately refrained from all activities, especially domestic, and solemnly communicated with their God. So, when Isaac could not get any response from his wife after calling her for about three times, he knew she had gone to pray. He knew she went to express her appreciation to God for the bundle of miracle and joy in her womb. Isaac therefore did not insist on reaching her no matter what. He was aware of what she might be doing so he smiled. Quietly, in his own small way, he also prayed, saying; Lord, may you incline your ears to the expression of her joy this afternoon. She had relied on you for a child all these years. And you have endowed her with not only a child, but twins after enduring the many insinuations thrown at her. You are the only one, LORD, that is capable to do that which you have done for her. I know your ears are not dull not to hear us but sometimes you delay so you will glorify you name. Though it had been tough for us, we relied on you and you performed mightily to take away our shame. May your name be forever praised, amen.

Isaac shook his head though. He was lying on that raw mat with his head on raised pillows. He had hardly finished saying amen this to his prayers when Rebekah's right foot stepped into their hut. She was bubbling over with this unusual joy. Isaac was enthralled by her commitment to their God. But Rebekah had her own version of excitement. And had come to express it to her beloved husband. She related to Isaac about her prayers this time. It was about the children jostling each other, and against the walls of her womb so, she went to enquire of the Lord the meaning of all this. Then the Lord, without hesitating, answered as recorded thus;

> The Lord said to her, "Two nations are in your womb, and two peoples from within you will be separated; one people will be stronger

than the other, and the older will serve the younger (Genesis 25:23).

She was so excited. She couldn't contain the subsequent joyful moments which followed. Vibrant life had returned to this once-dull abode. Continuous songs of worship and praise were heard from her lips. She was dripping with love, peace and perfect harmony. Rebekah had found her place among women in their small village. The days she bowed her head in shame were gone forever. The days she heard insinuations and innuendos, causing her life to be disorganized were things of the past now. The days she was vilified and humiliated among her neighbors for her inability to give birth were gone with history. She led a normal life like all previous women who gave birth to children in the village. Rebekah was blessed with the strength to carry her pregnancy to full term without any complications. She did all that was expected of her. And she was involved, performing activities beyond expectations. She went to farm, drew water from the stream and cooked her favorite meals.

Rebekah had been childless for many years after her marriage to Isaac. She did not take the challenge lightly then. It didn't sit well with her at all. It created unwanted tension between her and the husband. She attacked Isaac as if he held the keys to her closed womb. Note this, this family had once experienced contentious moments, escalating to unbearable dimensions. Times when Isaac's faith was tested and stretched to its maximum limit. Times when he was overwhelmed by the prevailing circumstances. On some occasions he doubted, to the extent of questioning the faith of his forefathers. He reacted in some unpleasant ways. His humanity was exposed. But in all, Isaac ultimately stood the test. And he prevailed. And whenever he remembered those trying times, he would then shake his head along with a smile. So, Rebekah's absence was not a surprise to him.

When the time was due for Rebekah to deliver, she gave birth to the twins as was promised by the Lord. They were named Esau and Jacob. Jacob was the youngest of the two. But he was cunny and deceptive. They grew beside each other. Life was normal in their family just like any other in their small village and neighborhood. Esau loved the fields; he was always in the bush hunting. He was also hairy, very distinct from his younger brother. On the other hand, Jacob was reserved and an introvert. Always at home and by the side of his beloved mother. Therefore, there was this strong bond that developed between and connected them to each other. For the love of the game Esau brought home, Isaac was also pulled toward and connected to his elder son. The father loved his son, and it was so clear and visible. Rebekah took Jacob's side. The Bible described the situation among them this way:

> The boys grew up, and Esau became a skillful hunter, a man of the open country, while Jacob was content to stay at home among the tents. Isaac, who had a taste for wild game, loved Esau, but Rebekah loved Jacob. (Genesis 25:27: 28)

Though it was not supposed to be so in any family, unfortunately so was the situation in this. The favoritism the parents displayed accentuated the sorry sibling rivalry between the boys. Yes, the parents took sides with their children, and it created a crack in the family dynamics. This crack in their family unity seemed not to bother anyone until calamity struck.

Esau had been married by now. And his marriage to the women added insult to injury. It was described thus,

> When Esau was forty years old, he married Judith daughter of Beeri the Hittite, and also Basemath daughter of Elon the Hittite. They were a source of grief to Isaac and Rebekah. (Genesis 26:24, 25)

The ensuing unfortunate instances exacerbated the fragile relationship between Esau's mother and her in-laws. Some bitter incidences surfaced once in a while, bringing unwarranted tensed moments to the family. But, despite all these, they managed to live with each other along the preferential line.

At this time Isaac was blind and therefore, was not as mobile as he used to be. Not as effective as he would have loved to be. Nature was taking its toll on him. He had lost his sight to old age. Yet he was proud of his twins, most especially Esau. Though the presence of these women in the life of Esau brought some rift in the family (Genesis 26:24,25), it did not anyway affect the relationship between Isaac and his first son, Esau. Rebekah expected her husband to support whatever grievances she might have raised. She sought it desperately so, they could gang up against the son's wives. Then they would be isolated, may be, causing changes in their lives. But unfortunately, the pendulum did not swing to her side. Isaac refused to buy into her idea. He was oblivious of the whole scheme. In her mind her husband did not care about how she was feeling. So, when Isaac called Esau that early morning and said;

> "…I am now an old man and don't know the day of my death. Now then, get your equipment - your quiver and bow - and go out to the open country to hunt some wild game for me. Prepare me the kind of tasty food I like and bring it to me to eat, so that I may give you my blessing before I die." (Genesis 27:2-4)

Rebekah was nearby eavesdropping the request the father made. She immediately made the decision to divert the blessing from Esau to Jacob. *"How was it going to happen?"* This would be the burning question everyone would want answers to. But to Rebekah the answer was not far away, and so she took this whole thing seriously. She would meticulously execute it to the letter. She left the scene without a sign or a trace of her presence. Esau, without the slightest idea his own mother would scheme against him, proudly collected his hunting gears, planted a powerful kiss on her cheeks, then waved her good-bye. He had not gone far when Rebekah located Jacob. Then without any hesitation,

> Rebekah said to her son Jacob, "Look, I overheard your father say to your brother Esau, 'Bring me some game and prepare me some tasty food to eat, so that I may give you my blessing in the presence of the Lord before I die.' Now, my son, listen carefully and do what I tell you: Go out to the flock and bring me two choice young goats, so I can prepare some tasty food for your father, just the way he likes it. Then take it to your father to eat, so that he may give you his blessing before he dies." (Genesis 27:6-10)

A plan was set in motion. Jacob stood there stunned by this sinister plan. So, he posed series of questions to the mother. Never in his wildest dreams would such a thought ever cross the mind of any intelligent person. He couldn't fathom himself standing before his father with a smooth skin when his elder brother was so hairy. "How could he beat the intelligence of the man who gave birth to him and watched him grow before his eyes?" This question and others hunted him as he stood in front of Rebekah. Should it backfire, he anticipated, his father would rain curses upon him instead of the blessing he sought. But a woman bent on achieving her aim would not stop at any opposition. So, Rebekah played down her son's concerns. And therefore, his concerns did not get any consideration. She must get through with her plans, and she did.

Jacob, who found it difficult to go along with the mother, reluctantly dragged his feet toward the pen. He stood at the gate for a few seconds as if to give the whole plan another thought before opening it. He then stepped in, grabbed the two young goats as requested by his mother and brought them to her. Though the goats were bleating so loudly, it did not anyway, deter Rebekah from retreating. She didn't rescind the decision she took but carried on with it. And in no time, the aroma of her sumptuous food pervaded the whole vicinity. She signaled Jacob to get ready to dress up for the blessings. She got Esau's hunting dress and gave it to Jacob. Then he carried the food to the father. The food had been quick in arriving so, he queried, "How did you find it so quickly, my son? and Jacob visibly trembling replied, "The Lord your God gave me success," he replied" (Genesis 27:20). "Yes, the Lord gave me success to find the game immediately," he said to ascertain the 'truth' he was telling his father. But Isaac doubted. He sensed deception right there and then. He was not convinced so he probed further for the truth. He asked Jacob to draw nearer so he could touch him. Jacob shook as he drew nearer to his father. Then Isaac leaned forward and touched this deceptive 'Esau' and blurted out his observation, "… 'The voice is the voice of Jacob, but the hands are the hands of Esau.'" (Genesis 27:22) Yet still, Isaac was not fully convinced. He couldn't trust the scene playing before him, but he needed to release his blessings to his son. "What should I do," he might have asked under this shadow of doubt. Therefore, he beckoned Jacob to come so he can kiss him.

> So he went to him and kissed him. When Isaac caught the smell of his clothes, he blessed him and said, "Ah, the smell of my son is like the smell of a field that the Lord has blessed. May God give you heaven's dew and earth's richness - an abundance of grain and new wine. May nations serve you and

peoples bow down to you. Be lord over your brothers, and may the sons of your mother bow down to you. May those who curse you be cursed and those who bless you be blessed." (Genesis 27:27-29)

Jacob, the pretender had once again usurped the blessings that belonged to his elder brother. Rebekah coerced her son to submit to her wicked machinations. Jacob could not persuade his mother from executing her plans so, he also bought into it and they outwitted the father. And Isaac, from the deepest part of his heart, bestowed the blessings upon Jacob. When Isaac had finished, Jacob lifted himself up, thanked the father and then walked away but,

> "…Jacob had scarcely left his father's presence, [when] his brother Esau came in from hunting. He too prepared some tasty food and brought it to his father. Then he said to him, "My father, please sit up and eat some of my game, so that you may give me your blessing." (Genesis 27:30,31)

Disappointed as he was, Esau sat in a corner of his father's hut and wept bitterly. He wept his hearts out.

No words were enough to console him. Then his father beckoned him to come. He drew nearer, and Isaac said to him,

> ..."Your dwelling will be away from the earth's richness, away from the dew of heaven above. You will live by the sword and you will serve your brother. But when you grow restless, you will throw his yoke from off your neck." (Genesis 27:39, 40)

Slowly and disappointedly, Esau dragged himself along to his place of abode. His face was cast down; he could not hold himself together. And the more he thought of it, the more his frustration boiled to the surface. There and then Esau resolved to take revenge on his brother. He hated him, he resented him, he begrudged him and was just waiting for the death of Isaac so, he could square it off with Jacob. Someone got wind of his intentions and passed the information on to Rebekah. As a mother, she was bothered. She was concerned and therefore alerted Jacob to prepare and run away to safety. The Bible narrated the episode that;

> When Rebekah was told what her older son Esau had said, she sent for her younger son

Jacob and said to him, "Your brother Esau is planning to avenge himself by killing you. Now then, my son, do what I say: Flee at once to my brother Laban in Harran. Stay with him for a while until your brother's fury subsides. When your brother is no longer angry with you and forgets what you did to him, I'll send word for you to come back from there. Why should I lose both of you in one day?" (Genesis 27:42-45)

Thus, Jacob outwitted his brother once again, leaving him in limbo. Esau's intention to avenge the deceits of his younger brother could not be realized. The orchestration could not materialize. His world came crashing down. Esau and Jacob would thus be separated, for how long, no one knew. But Esau had to live and he lived with it.

Apology Rendered

Time, it is said, heals wounds. And this analogy had been subjected to scrutiny over time. But it's found to be true only in cases where the offended victim received apology, and restitution where necessary. So, we can truly affirm this analogy if it is preceded by sincere apology to the offended person.

Otherwise, the wound would just dry on the surface leaving severe pain underneath. Though the words, "apology" and/or "I'm sorry," had not visibly appeared in Esau and Jacob's narrative, they could be seen. These words were sincerely expressed through Jacob's approach to the feud.

Many years had passed now since Jacob fleeced his elder brother through the mother's initiatives and robbed him of his blessings. A lot happened during this period and correspondingly, a lot changed in the lives of these brothers. These brothers were not kids anymore. They had become matured in many ways: their thinking had changed, the perspective from which life is viewed had altered and the thirst for new relationship with each other had metamorphosed into something different. They were looking forward to meeting each other as reality had set in. Time had had tremendous effect on them though they were miles apart. And it was manifested in the way they reacted when they came face to face.

Jacob bolted away to his mother's family. The intention was to evade Esau's wrath. He succeeded. He arrived and was welcomed with open arms. Jacob fell in love with Rachel, the second daughter of his uncle Laban. He expressed his interest in the girl to the uncle. His request was accepted. To pay for the dowry, he was asked to work for seven years. He did the work and was ready to receive Rachel as his bride. But the night he was to consummate the marriage, he was tricked by his father-in-law. Laban gave away Leah the elder sister of Rachel. Jacob was hurt for this deception and complained bitterly. Then,

> Laban replied, "It is not our custom here to give the younger daughter in marriage before the older one. Finish this daughter's bridal week; then we will give you the younger one also, in return for another seven years of work." (Genesis 29:26, 27)

It was suggested to Jacob to work another seven years for Rachel. He realized he could not overturn their customs and he loved her. He immediately accented the suggestion and struck a deal with the in-laws. So, "…he worked for Laban another seven years" for Rachel. His love for her was so great that the years passed by in no time. Rachel became a second wife and she was loved more. As a result, the Lord closed her womb. The unloved Leah gave birth to six boys at the time when Rachel had one in addition to her servant's child.

Jacob amassed great wealth by this time and planned to return home, the same home he left abruptly to avoid vengeance from his elder brother. He was embarking on a mission to mend fences and to make wrong things right with those whom he offended along the way. He was not deterred but encouraged to fulfil his mission. He moved with precision and decisiveness to get it right. In a bid to obviate the tension created through his shrewd behaviors, he enacted a plan. Jacob assembled his servants. He laid before them how he wanted to approach Esau in order not to arouse his anger. To begin with,

> Jacob sent messengers ahead of him to his brother Esau in the land of Seir, the country of Edom. He instructed them: "This is what you are to say to my lord Esau: 'Your servant Jacob says, I have been staying with Laban and have remained there till now. I have cattle and donkeys, sheep and goats, male and female servants. Now I am sending this message to my lord, that I may find favor in your eyes.'" (Genesis 32:3-5)

When he had finished with his instructions, he divided them into groups. Then he specifically repeated the messages they were supposed to carry to his elder brother to each one. The Bible says,

> He instructed the one in the lead: "When my brother Esau meets you and asks, 'Who do you belong to, and where are you going, and who owns all these animals in front of you?' then you are to say, 'They belong to <u>your servant Jacob</u>. They are a gift sent to my lord Esau, and he is coming behind us.'" (Genesis 32: 17, 18)

The first group had hardly gone far when Jacob - on a mission to accept responsibility for all that transpired between them, render apology and then extend a hand for forgiveness - moved toward the second and the subsequent groups. The narrator described the scene thus;

> He also instructed the second, the third and all the others who followed the herds: "You are to say the same thing to Esau when you meet him. And be sure to say, '<u>Your servant Jacob</u> is coming behind us.'" For he thought, "I will <u>pacify</u> him with these gifts I am

sending on ahead; later, when I see him, perhaps he will receive me." So Jacob's gifts went on ahead of him, but he himself spent the night in the camp (Genesis 32:19-21).

With his entire family standing beside him, he looked on as the sight of the messengers going ahead faded away. He was tensed. He played it over in his mind how Esau might act when they meet. Then Jacob bowed a little bit and said this prayer to lift his discouraged spirit up:

> I lift up my eyes to the mountains - where does my help come from? My help comes from the Lord, the Maker of heaven and earth. He will not let your foot slip - he who watches over you will not slumber; indeed, he who watches over Israel will neither slumber nor sleep. The Lord watches over you - the Lord is your shade at your right hand; the sun will not harm you by day, nor the moon by night. The Lord will keep you from all harm - he will watch over your life; the Lord will watch over your coming and going both now and forevermore (Psalm 121:1-8).

Jacob was gripped with fear, fears that stemmed from a conscience that had been guilty from the get-go. Fear had paralyzed him. He could not cast it off. He was matured now and realized he shouldn't have threaded that path. But the offence had already been committed and the past could not be changed. However, he has the prerogative now to create a better future for himself and his brother. So, slowly he walked behind not knowing what to expect. But "The king's heart is in the hand of the LORD;..." (Proverbs 21:1). Far away, when he lifted his eyes, he saw Esau and his men coming toward them at a terrific speed. Then he panicked. But the scene played differently. The scene unraveling before him was overwhelming as Esau's men rushed toward him. When he recognized Jacob,

> ...Esau ran to meet Jacob and embraced him; he threw his arms around his neck and kissed him. And they wept. Then Esau looked up and saw the women and children. "Who are these with you?" he asked. Jacob answered, "They are the children God has graciously given your servant" (Genesis 33:4, 5).

FOOD FOR THOUGHT

- What do you think would have happened if Jacob did not approach Esau with the intention to pacify him?

- What do you think would have happened if Jacob threw his weight around to justify what he did to Esau?

- What do you think would have been Esau's reaction toward Jacob if he did throw his weight around?

- Do you think Jacob's approach contributed to the amicable solution to the feud?

Chapter 2
MY FAILURE
David and Uriah

"Create in me a pure heart, O God, and renew a steadfast spirit within me. Do not cast me from your presence or take your Holy Spirit from me. Restore to me the joy of your salvation and grant me a willing spirit, to sustain me." (Psalm 51:10-12)

"Apology is the glue that sticks broken pieces of forgiveness together. It doesn't matter how far those pieces might have gone." (Author)

The prophet had just finished with his parable. And the king fumed with rage. He disdained this evil person who - though in a good position to provide for his guest - used his privilege to rob the neighbor. A man who perpetrated a crime David did not feel shy to show his contempt for. Fury undergirded the words dripping from his mouth. And he spewed this anger in every direction. David could not catch his breath as he was so incensed by the attitude of this evil person. The prophet Nathan stood there looking at a man who had no inclination he was the transgressor in the prophet's parable. Nathan ascribed such cruelty to this person. He made his case against this miscreant eloquently, choosing the right form of presentation to give the message no denial. He crafted it well and the message penetrated perfectly. So, "David burned with anger against the man and said to Nathan, "As surely as the Lord lives, the man who did this must die!"" (2 Samuel 12:5). He expressed his disapproval for this heinous act. If the felon - whom David never perceived it to be him but someone else - was standing before him, he would have done something cruel and senseless. He would have charged his guards to deal with him in a way to send message to the whole land. The king ranted and raged while the prophet waited patiently. He was so upset. And when David had calmed down after his diatribe, Nathan cleared his throat and stood up from the seat offered him by the servants. He drew nearer to the center in the king's palace hall and began to explain the meaning of his parable to the king.

The prophet seized the opportunity to inform the king of his mission to the palace at this odd time of the day. That the Lord had sent him to deliver a message to him. King David sat on his throne with rapt attention. He was curious to know the content of the message. Nathan, matured and astute at his calling as a prophet, began to explain the parable. The whole palace became quiet. This quiet scene played before their eyes as the prophet explained every sentence. He was slow in speaking but meticulous. His narrative touched nerves and raised eyebrows. When he had looked straight into the eyes of the king those tragic words fell, "Now, therefore, the sword will never depart from your house, because you despised me and took the wife of Uriah the Hittite to be your own.'" (2 Samuel 12:10) Then the shameful king, who did everything to coverup his acts, reacted soberly in response. The calm atmosphere was punctured by shock and awe. It was a very difficult moment to behold.

Offence Committed

The kingdom just witnessed the worst winter in her history. It had really been cold, and every citizen of the kingdom felt it to the core. This feeling went as far as the palace. There were indications all over the kingdom they were not happy about the season. In fact, it was everyone's desire that it went away as early as possible. But the inconveniences that came along with this uncomfortable situation dragged on, going away rather slowly. So, the first sign of spring was hailed with joy amid ecstasy. It meant they must begin the preparation toward reclaiming lands that had been encroached upon by others. Kings at this moment looked forward to this time so they can take their subjects to wars. King David was no exception. His kingdom would not be excluded. Therefore, he sent words to all commanders to alert the soldiers of the impending wars.

King David participated in many military campaigns defeating all his enemies. The hand of God was upon him so He "...delivered your enemies into your hand" (Genesis 14:20). David enjoyed the favor of God and basked in His glory throughout his days as king. He loved the Lord and obeyed Him. As vulnerable and deceitful as he was, scheming his way through scandals, David's heart was for God. He never deserted the Lord in any moment, even in times when he had fumbled the most. Those were the times he drew nearer to his Maker the most to plead for mercy. So, to allow his commander Joab to lead the campaign this spring was not, in anyway, an issue to be considered. The anointing of God was upon him. He released it to Joab who was acting on his behalf. He would go on to win victory.

It was war time and he should have been thinking of his men, men who sacrificed their lives to be at war front. But this conviction that the hand of God was so great in his life, made him to take this afternoon nap. When he had had enough sleep, David woke up to parade the corridors of his palace. He strolled back and forth. He never gave thought to anything special. Out of nowhere, he saw this beautiful woman bathing. He lusted after her. The king did not hesitate to send someone to enquire about her. In no time, the messenger came back with an answer. "The man said, 'She is Bathsheba, the daughter of Eliam and the wife of Uriah the Hittite.'" (2 Samuel 11:3) This response should have convinced the king to abort the whole plan, but he refused to budge. This compelled king Solomon to query rhetorically:

> Can a man scoop fire into his lap without his clothes being burned? Can a man walk on hot coals without his feet being scorched? So is he who sleeps with another man's wife; no one who touches her will go unpunished. (Proverbs 6:27-29)

Job, determined not to violate his covenant with God, responded saying, "I made a covenant with my eyes not to look lustfully at a young woman..." (Job 31:1). With all this, David continued unheeded, resolved to achieve his aim. He was bent on getting what he wanted and would get it through any means, even foul. Every effort to persuade him from pursuing this agendum could not materialize. He resisted vehemently, reminding the folks he was the king.

David sent for Bathsheba, Uriah's wife. He desired so much to satisfy this craving, he wouldn't take no for an answer.

He pursued her unashamedly and slept with her. This offensive act went on when Bathsheba's dedicated husband was at the war front fighting for his beloved country. What a betrayal of trust from a leader! From a leader of David's caliber, a man after God's own heart. A stab at the back. A few weeks had not passed when Bathsheba related to the king that her condition had changed. Then, "The woman conceived and sent word to David, saying, "I am pregnant"" (2 Samuel 11:5). This news came as a shock to the king. A volcano was about to erupt. He became hysterical and jittery, confused and awed, yet he repudiated her claim. As a result, he didn't waste time to dig for more information. However, his worst fears were confirmed when the messenger came back with the damaging news. Immediately, the king sensed danger lurking at his doorsteps. The consequences for his skirmishes would be so devastating should they be made public. The king realized the brunt of this shameful act would be too big a burden for him to carry. So, he decided to move fast to curtail the spreading news of this dalliance of his.

> Do not plot harm against your neighbor, who lives trustfully near you. Do not accuse anyone for no reason - when they have done you no harm." (Proverbs 3:29, 30)

This warning never rang a bell in David's ears. With all these cautions, he decided to move. What was the first move David made to protect his image? Nothing but attempts to push Uriah to his wife.

> So David sent this word to Joab: "Send me Uriah the Hittite." And Joab sent him to David. When Uriah came to him, David asked him how Joab was, how the soldiers were and how the war was going. Then David said to Uriah, "Go down to your house and wash your feet." So Uriah left the palace, and a gift from the king was sent after him. But Uriah slept at the entrance to the palace with all his master's servants and did not go down to his house. (2 Samuel 11:6-9)

David's intentions were that Uriah would go to sleep with his wife then the pregnancy would be pinned on him. But it was to no avail. Every effort to make Uriah compromise his orchestrations proved futile. David went to the extent of threatening to send Uriah back to the war front. His patriotism, commitment and love for the country were above the threats so Uriah was not shaken. He mustered courage to defy the king's threats. Uriah went against the king's directives. When David could not succeed, he sent Uriah back to the military campaign going on. Uriah, patriotic as he was, obeyed the king and went back. As Uriah was ready to leave,

> In the morning David wrote a letter to Joab and sent it with Uriah. In the letter he wrote, "Put Uriah out in front where the fighting is fiercest. Then withdraw from him so he will be struck down and die." (2 Samuel 11:14, 15)

Uriah carried in his own hands a letter to Joab, the commander; a letter that warranted his death. And he carried it with respect and love for his country, and dedication and commitment to his king. Yet king David decided to badly reward Uriah with this diabolic plan, just because he wanted to save face. Joab condoned the king's designs. So, when the battle escalated to its fiercest point and,

> ...while Joab had the city under siege, he put Uriah at a place where he knew the strongest defenders were. When the men of the city came out and fought against Joab, some of the men in David's army fell; moreover, Uriah the Hittite died. (2 Samuel 11: 16, 17)

This young man, a dear husband and a good father, fighting on behalf of the country he so loved lost his life tragically and prematurely. At the prime of his life when the whole world was opened ahead of him with immeasurable opportunities. So, when it happened, Joab sent a quick appraisal of the battle to the king. Unfortunately, he included the demise of Uriah in his missive. When he came to deliver the message,

> The messenger said to David, "The men overpowered us and came out against us in the open, but we drove them back to the entrance of the city gate. Then the archers shot arrows at your servants from the wall, and some of the king's men died. Moreover, your servant Uriah the Hittite is dead (2 Samuel 11: 23, 24).

David was elated. That heavy weight hanging over him had been lifted. He thought he'd succeeded in achieving his plans to cover the escapade. He believed by eliminating Uriah, he would tamp down the rumor mills, but it did not work. On the other side of the fence tragedy had hit home; a tragedy that could have been averted if the king showed class and resisted just a little bit. If the king thought of his dignity, the result would have been otherwise. Therefore, "When Uriah's wife heard that her husband was dead, she mourned for him" (2 Samuel 11:26). A writer quoting, with reference to similar situation, says

> Dietrich Bonhoeffer made the observation that when lust takes control, "At this moment God…loses all reality…Satan does not fill us with hatred of God, but with the forgetfulness of God." (Hughes, 1991)

By this adulterous act, David smeared decency with deception, decorum with disdain. David descended to the lowest level as he lost his own identity. He treated the word of God contemptuously, despising its essence and worth. Rationality was scattered in all directions and civility lost its core value with him at this moment. In that small world of his, David thought he'd gotten away with this distasteful action. *"I've eluded everyone,"* he might have thought because of the pervading silence, but not God. Though God was silent at this moment, it would not last forever. Peter, reminding us of God's patience, said we should

> … not forget this one thing, dear friends: With the Lord a day is like a thousand years, and a thousand years are like a day. The Lord

is not slow in keeping his promise, as some understand slowness. Instead he is patient with you, not wanting anyone to perish, but everyone to come to repentance. (2 Peter 3:8-9)

Little did he know God was at his heels. That He would pursue him to a logical conclusion. The day of reckoning was drawing nearer by the tick of the clock. With that David never thought of any impending indictment. The loud silence over the issue gave him boldness to act further. As a result, after the mourning period for her beloved husband was over, Bathsheba was brought to David in the palace and she became his wife. She came along with the son she bore for him from the pregnancy that culminated in the death of Uriah. David's life went contrary to the confidence God imposed on him. Luke recorded a prior testimony about David that,

After removing Saul, he made David their king. God testified concerning him: 'I have found David son of Jesse, a man after my own heart; he will do everything I want him to do.' (Acts 13:22)

Unfortunately, David could not live up to this testimony. He greatly disappointed God, who entrusted His people into his hands. As a leader, the protection for the flocks should not have been in conflict with his personal desires yet, he did allow. Jesus warned that,

> ... Everyone who hears these words of mine and puts them into practice is like a wise man who built his house on the rock. The rain came down, the streams rose, and the winds blew and beat against that house; yet it did not fall, because it had its foundation on the rock. But everyone who hears these words of mine and does not put them into practice is like a foolish man who built his house on sand. The rain came down, the streams rose, and the winds blew and beat against that house, and it fell with a great crash. (Matthew 7:24-27)

With all these warnings, David could not still control himself. He went on to act the way he wanted to.

But God would act accordingly and swiftly without, in any way, compromising His holiness on the altar of irresponsibility.

Apology Rendered

With the absence of any complaint against David of his infidelity with Bathsheba and the delivery of their son, calm returned to the palace and to the king. No one was bold or courageous enough to confront the king about his actions. Yes, no one raised any finger nor did any rumor surrounding the escapade reached the king's ears. So, in the interim, he had gotten away with it. With that, life returned to normalcy and happenings seemed to be moving in the right direction. Every inhabitant of the city, and those beyond were fully engaged with their businesses. There was no sign God would move. And it never occurred to David there would be any indictment against him so, he continued his illicit relationship with Bathsheba. A relationship built on a murderous foundation. But a thick cloud was forming, and a storm gathering was about to be unleashed. They were moving at a terrific speed towards the palace. No one anticipated the palace to be their destination. And it was going to wreak havoc beyond recognition. When they land no defensive mechanism would be able to avert their impact.

David just got out of bed and made his way to the bathroom, so he could prepare for the day's activities. The day had no event of any royal significance. The king, therefore, was not in a hurry to attend to the few issues in the palace. And Prophet Nathan was not expected too. But heaven does not need to make any appointment with anyone. Wherever God's presence was needed, there He goes to do what he was supposed to. Bathsheba, the newest among the numerous wives, was on schedule to prepare the king's food for the day. So, for the king's thinly scattered agenda, Bathsheba was also not under pressure to get David to the table for breakfast. She took her time to bake bread, get the herbs and the lentil stew for breakfast. When all was set, she instructed one of the palace servants to alert the king breakfast was ready. Without wasting time, this servant disappeared to inform David. At this time, the king was, coincidentally, standing at the spot where he stood to see Bathsheba. Slowly, he dragged himself to the table as a response to the wife's call.

David sat at the royal dining table with majesty and pomp. There was a display of power, privilege, splendor and magnificence. The kingdom was enjoying peace never seen or heard of before. David was hailed wherever he went to. His subjects adored him and were proud to serve under his leadership. He was the killer of Goliath, that Philistine soldier who taunted the army of God. A hero of all time. No one surpasses his tall achievements. His life seemed to be well organized. But David's world was about to tumble down. There was going to be a shake or a shift in the palace's arrangements.

The atmosphere at the palace this time was serene. Some unimagined calmness had invaded the palace that morning. The king had just a few cases to take care of so there was enough time to chat with his elders. Their conversation stretched over a long span of time. They never considered time flying by so quickly. Then the ecstasy that engulfed their presence was broken. A palace gatekeeper came rushing to inform the king and his elders of the prophet's presence. The prophet was coming without following any proper royal protocol. It looked like he was intruding upon the king. However, David welcomed him warmly. Nathan paid the king homage. The servants provided a seat for him but chose to stand. King David was taken aback by this solemn refusal. Immediately, the king wanted to know what might have brought the prophet to the palace at this odd hour of the day.

While he was still standing, Nathan decided to deliver his message. He shrouded it all in a parable. Then

> ...He said, "There were two men in a certain town, one rich and the other poor. The rich man had a very large number of sheep and cattle, but the poor man had nothing except one little ewe lamb he had bought. He raised it, and it grew up with him and his children. It shared his food, drank from his cup and even slept in his arms. It was like a daughter to him. "Now a traveler came to the rich man, but the rich man refrained from taking one of his own sheep or cattle to prepare a meal for the traveler who had come to him. Instead, he took the ewe lamb that belonged to the poor man and prepared it for the one who had come to him." (2 Samuel 12:1-4)

The prophet paused abruptly so he could gather some breath and clear his dried throat. He gestured, then he took two steps towards the king. With all eyes fixed on him, the prophet looked straight at the king. And that look touched nerves, inviting a deep silence and acute attention. At this time David's demeanor changed drastically and he burned with fury. The king's face reddened, and he shook visibly with great hurt in his voice. "This is despicable," the king aptly suggested. Looking at him, his eyes blazed with immeasurable anger and untamed fury. He expressed his utmost disgust towards this rich man. A perpetrator who failed to heed this golden call:

> Do nothing out of selfish ambition or vain conceit. Rather, in humility value others above yourselves, not looking to your own interests but each of you to the interests of the others. (Philippians 2:3,4)

He had no regards for his fellow human being. No pity at all. And it's imperative he must pay and as well, pay four times for what he robbed from the poor man. It was sobering for the prophet to hear such suggestion from the ignorant perpetrator's own mouth. And so, he continued with the message he was to deliver. He spoke harshly, pointing

> ...To David, "You are the man! This is what the Lord, the God of Israel, says: 'I anointed you king over Israel, and I delivered you from the hand of Saul. I gave your master's house to you, and your master's wives into your arms. I gave you all Israel and Judah. And if

all this had been too little, I would have given
you even more. Why did you despise the word
of the Lord by doing what is evil in his eyes?
You struck down Uriah the Hittite with the
sword and took his wife to be your own. You
killed him with the sword of the Ammonites.
(2 Samuel 12:7-9)

With these words falling from the prophet's mouth,
David trembled terribly to the core. The content of
the narrative left him crippled. Crippled by
destitution and devastation. It left him embarrassed,
humiliated and defeated. Immediately, king David
became frail and vulnerable. He realized his image
would be in tatters beyond redemption. Shame
enveloped him so much that he couldn't utter a
word for a considerable time. Suffice it to say, the
news later spread like a wildfire. And there was no
way it could have been controlled. In a humble tone,
the prophet passed the judgment of God, saying;

Now, therefore, the sword will never depart
from your house, because you despised me
and took the wife of Uriah the Hittite to be
your own. (2 Samuel 12:10)

As if that was the final seal to God's deal with him, Nathan went on further to deliver the consequences David would face. The Bible narrated the situation thus:

> "This is what the Lord says: 'Out of your own household I am going to bring calamity on you. Before your very eyes I will take your wives and give them to one who is close to you, and he will sleep with your wives in broad daylight. You did it in secret, but I will do this thing in broad daylight before all Israel'" (2 Samuel 12:11, 12).

A pin-drop silence invaded the palace. For a period, time seemed to have stood still. Confusion would have been understatement. The prophet's final pronouncement ripped him into shreds. David sat there stone-cold, awed and perplexed. There was no way he could have feigned his demeanor. There was no way he could or would have defended himself, but to admit his guilt and accept the verdict. The evidence mounted was so strong, he had no window of escape or excuse. By this time, this powerful king, without any equal, was paralyzed from a revelation he never anticipated would be in the public domain. In an instant, David recognized his humanity and frailty. How culpable he was. How imperfect we are. So, in a loud but a humble cry unto the Lord, "… David said to Nathan, "I have sinned against the Lord…"" (2 Samuel 12:13a). By this admission, the king unequivocally accepted responsibility for his actions.

Those words mirrored the contents of his heart as he sat there. He felt remorseful. Those words echoed David's regret for what he did to Uriah and his family. The devastation he brought upon this poor and peaceful family. Had Uriah been alive then, David would have personally extended a hand of apology. He was ready to mend fence had the possibility been there. His sincerity was, therefore, not doubted; never called into question. David owned up to this detestable and disturbing crime he committed, not only against his fellow man, but God above. But then God, who knows what is going on in a man's heart, detected the genuineness of David's. This happened to prove right when God said we, "People look at the outward appearance, but the Lord looks at the heart." (1 Samuel 16:7b) He saw David's regret in his words. Many questions flooded his mind. Questions that practically begged for answers. To assure him, "…Nathan replied, 'The

Lord has taken away your sin. You are not going to die.'" (2 Samuel 12:13b)

FOOD FOR THOUGHT

- What do you think would have happened if David's schemes were not discovered?
- What do you think would have been the reaction of the folks in the palace if David had denied?
- What would have been David's fate for his despicable crime against Uriah if his denial had been successful?
- How would have events turned out if David did not say, 'I have sinned," for his crimes?

Chapter 3
MY UNWORTHINESS
The Father and his Prodigal Son

"When he came to his senses, he said, 'How many of my father's hired servants have food to spare, and here I am starving to death! I will set out and go back to my father and say to him: Father, I have sinned against heaven and against you. I am no longer worthy to be called your son; make me like one of your hired servants.' So he got up and went to his father..." (Luke 15:17-20)

"Apology is like a substance that speeds up the reaction of forgiveness in the crucible of conflict. No matter how hard forgiveness might be apology softens it." (Author)

The old man had no strong spine to accept the words that just fell from his second son's mouth. So shocked that he sat up immediately. "You must be joking," the father shot back at his son, Sammy. But when he patiently lifted his head up and looked at those piercing eyes of his son, immediately he acknowledged the seriousness of his words. For he realized it wasn't a joke as he thought it to be. The father then, quickly dispatched Sammy from his presence. He was amazed by this damned demand from his son. Sammy's mere request for his share of the inheritance was an affront to the father within the context of the Jewish culture, most especially when he was still alive. He tried to convince himself this was just one of his jokes. But every attempt to brush aside what he just experienced couldn't materialized from that moment onwards. It kept coming back instead. It'd captured his attention and held him captive. He couldn't shake off this short interaction with his son. It hunted him till his wife would return from seeing their neighbors.

At the gate, the wife began to call out her husband. Brimming with optimism, she expected the usual response from her husband, but was not forth coming. She entered the compound in a state of skepticism. "What is going on with this silence?" bewildered wife quizzed no one in particular. Quickly, she dashed to where her husband was used to resting. And to her surprise, he was holed up in that corner completely puzzled. He was so confused and out of this world. The reason, which she couldn't perceive, was the attitude her second son displayed just a few moments ago.

This rich father of Sammy had a retinue of servants in his household. As a routine, they took orders for what they were supposed to do for the week. And since that day was the beginning of the week, they were there for their usual weekly orders. He woke up early so that, together with the group leaders, they could map out schedules for the servants. It had been this way for all those years, therefore, this exercise went on smoothly. The gathering dispersed, with the noise accompanying their departure going very far. They left to their various posts: the kitchen, the gate, the farm and so on.

When he was left alone, the father beckoned his business partners, who were waiting for him, to come for their weekly meetings. For no apparent reason, that day's business meeting dragged on for more than was expected, depriving the host access to his lunch time. So, he famished. His wife couldn't contain the delay so, she passed by several times to draw the attention of the partners. However, every attempt she made did not attract the attention of those business folks. They were so immersed in the transactions and negotiations going on nothing seemed to bother them. It was not too long after the ninth attempt when they concluded all they had to discuss. Quickly, he saw them off and dashed towards the meal waiting for him. His dear wife sat by and chatted with him. In course of their conversation, which was about nothing so special, his wife remembered she promised their neighbors a visit. She picked herself up and left at a lightning speed.

The father had just finished eating and wanted to rest for a few minutes before proceeding to do something else. He cleared his throat and relaxed, leaning solemnly against the big tree providing shade to the family. He was drifting into a nap when his younger son intruded upon him with his plan. So young and so ignorant, he never endeavored to consider the ramifications of his idea. Those words just fell off sending his father into a deep thought.

So deep, he couldn't notice his wife presence. It was in this mood that his wife found him. "What had kept you so occupied that you could not respond to my calls," she gently enquired. Then he beckoned her to come and hear what Sammy had brought to bear on them. He narrated what transpired in her absence.

Offence Committed

Sammy's father was pacing up and down their small porch waiting for a cry from the adjacent room. He was anxious and, it was taking a toll on him. It was visible. When one of the women attending to the laboring mother came out from the room to pick a piece of cloth, he dashed to her to update himself with what was going on. When she had gotten what she came out for, she took her time and thoroughly explained to him all that was transpiring behind the door. Nodding his head in response to all that was being said, the woman began her walk back to the room. A few minutes had just passed when the baby raised a cry to signal a safe arrival. Sammy, the second son to this family had been born. Sammy's conception caused a stir in the community.

The nine-month journey had come to an end. A moment of celebration had dawned. The boy they looked for, culminating in having those unplanned six girls, finally came. Sammy's father could not hide his joy. However, it opened another chapter of their lives, raising him in the fear of the Lord. He signaled their neighbors to join in the celebration. They didn't disappoint him. They responded in droves. This went on deep into the night before finally they dispersed to their various homes. According to the attending midwives, mother and child were doing fine. There was no cause for alarm as far as their health was concerned. Their condition therefore, did not encourage the few relatives to stay for long. They all returned home in no time.

The preparation had reached feverish pitch. The community was in frenzy. The community was in good mood to celebrate with Sammy's family. They counted every second as the clock ticked them. Every second was important since many things were outlined to be done for this day. Sammy was experiencing a mixed feeling of joy and anxiety. It was his day and time to celebrate this event, the Bar Mitzvah. This is a Jewish custom performed to initiate a male child into adulthood. A time when it's announced to the whole world that a son had come of age. And from that day onwards, that son would begin to be held accountable for his actions. It is done at the age of thirteen. And Sammy would be one of the young lads to be initiated. But Sammy's stood out for many reasons. His father was rich and would be celebrated with a spectacular display of wealth. For many years, he was the son the father had been looking for. And finally, he was the last of the only two sons his father had among the crop of kids borne to him.

It was widely known in the community that Sammy was a pampered child. He was swollen-headed, proud and oftentimes, disrespectful and snobbish. Whatever he needed was just a flip of fingers and a few seconds away from him. A child that was denied nothing. Sammy took advantage of the freedom granted him to drive his parents and siblings crazy. He went everywhere he wanted to with no one to enforce any proper rule. The admonishing, "Train a child in the way he should go, and when he is old he will not turn from it" seemed to have lost its meaning when it came to Sammy. (Proverbs 22:6) He set his own parameters and operated within it without any qualms.

This young man lived his life like a sheep without a shepherd. He followed his instinct wherever it took him to. Instead of leaning on reasoning, his instinct took the upper hand and dictated the pace. It was through one of such outings that Sammy met someone who would introduce him to a world beyond theirs out there to be explored. It was this acquaintance who raised the lad's hopes of a better life away from home.

Sammy, being so naïve and ignorant, bought into all the deceptions. In his small world, he believed the grass was greener on the other side. He was driven crazy by the fantasies painted in his mind. He played and dreamed about it, day in and day out. He couldn't resist anymore the lure of this imagined world out there. Based on these outrageous lies, he set out to plan how he could gather funds to finance his adventure. Sammy careened around many ideas, eliminating those he thought were not feasible. He even sought suggestions from a few friends who were close to him. After careful thought, he concluded there was no other way around to go but the father. He settled on the idea to request for his share of the father's property. And finally, he made the move.

Sammy chose that moment, a moment when his father was all by himself. To ascertain that the father was not deeply asleep, Sammy threw a big stone against their bamboo fence. His father's gesture confirmed his intentions; he shifted, and Sammy knew his father wasn't asleep. He would therefore, give him a hearing. Then he approached the father and, Sammy being, "The younger one said to his father, 'Father, give me my share of the estate...'" (Luke 15:12a) The father met these words with utmost shock as its waves climbed up his spine. He couldn't sit straight anymore after experiencing that shock. Sammy saw denial in those protruding eyes of his father's. The anger displayed told the whole story. But this young man was not deterred, he pushed further. After blatantly refusing to grant him this bogus request, Sammy's father dismissed him from his presence. When his mother heard the story, she took it for a joke.

A few days had not passed when Sammy approached the father again. This time in the presence of his mother to press home his demands. It was at this juncture she realized the seriousness her son attached to what he was looking for. This prompted her to act quickly to avert any disaster or disgrace his actions might bring upon the family. For that reason, she solicited assistance from uncles and aunties, nieces and nephews, friends and family but to no avail. She went as far as the chief of their small town and their synagogue ruler if that would help to change his mind. "Honor your father and your mother, so that you may live long in the land the LORD your God is giving you." (Exodus 20:12) The synagogue ruler once said to him. But Sammy resisted all efforts. He stood just where he had been and wouldn't move an inch. This went on for over three months, and with each passing day, he was emboldened to act.

One day, his father sat him down and said all that was to be. Finally, he looked directly and squarely into those young eyes; softly and solemnly spoke this few words: "There is a way that appears to be right, but in the end it leads to death." (Proverbs 14:16) The father hoped it would break the camel's back, but it never worked. Considering the prominent people involved in all attempts, and the threats from Sammy and his hired thugs, the father gave up hope. He succumbed to the son's request.

Prevailing circumstances compelled the father to do that which was against norms and values of the society. There was no other way but this. "...So he divided his property between them." (Luke 15:12b) But he did it with swollen pains in his heart since he knew the consequences involved when parents are disobeyed. But happily, Sammy put his share of the properties together. Then he designed how to embark on this journey to nowhere. He disposed of almost all the shares he got, put all proceeds together and set a date he would say goodbye to his family.

Sammy planned everything meticulously and was ready any time for this adventure he fantasized about for the past several months. He assured himself of success and would come back later to display his acquired wealth. At least, that ideal perception had not faded when he fell asleep that night. Early in the morning, "Not long after that, the younger son got together all he had, set off for a distant country..." (Luke 15:13a)

Apology Rendered

Sammy arrived with naivety and ignorance about the big city and its vibrant life. No one took the time to thoroughly explained to him the intrigues of city life. Though he possessed that disadvantage, one thing was sure, he had cash. And with that bundles of money in his possession everything was possible. He proudly assured himself. It took quite some days for him to settle into mainstream life. There were glitz and glamor displayed everywhere, of which he had not set his eyes on before. Sammy was a champion in their small town, hailed and held in high esteem. But over here, the environment was different and so were the dynamics. Therefore, he was required to adjust to these new conditions. And the change must be rapid since city life moves in a fast pace. His whole appearance and demeanor announced loudly his was a new arrival in town. He saw and peacefully admitted to it. The first attempt was to overhaul his wardrobe, so he could fit in. And he did it with assistance from his first acquaintance, the hotel's doorkeeper.

Not too long after Sammy's arrival, he gained popularity and notoriety, all through his money. Soon he got a few friends who would introduce him to the hot spots around the city. He frequented these spots in the company of these friends. With the stack of cash, the tab was always pinned on Sammy. For the sake of fame, he never for once complained. Also, he never bothered to check whatever bill that was handed to him. And so, it was with tips. He would dip the hand into his pocket or the wallet, whatever he laid his hands on went out as tip. With these numerous friends trailing him, he went to brothels and enjoyed himself to the fullest. He cut loose and was not stoppable. This kind of lifestyle went on without stopping one day to appraise his life. His influence over the folks who followed him was unprecedented, so this kind of life went on daily.

By the time Sammy would realize to take stock of his life, he'd been to a lot of these hot spots "…and there squandered his wealth in wild living." (Luke 15:13b) Now he was short on cash, and there was no one to turn to. The lifestyle he enjoyed in this foreign land reached its ceiling. Difficulty invaded his already-scattered life and hit him hard like a thunderbolt. Home beckoned him, but it was far away. To alleviate the situation and assuage his pain, he began to sell off some of his possessions: the jewelry, the sound systems, dresses, pieces of furniture and anything that could be sold. Finally, he sold the last of his fleet of cars. Sammy Young, as he was popular called because of his youthful appearance, began to fade away. His popularity was waning by the day and losing the many friends in droves. The quest for want now heavily dawned on him.

At this point, Sammy was living on the fringe of depravity having lost all. Life had become unbearable for him. He had no idea what he was supposed to do. He moved out of the mansion he acquired and rented a small room to suffice the little left in hand. No sooner, he couldn't meet the rent bill. The bill was piling upon each other, until the landlord couldn't take any more excuses. The next action, he was threatened with, was eviction. Nothing but hope was the last straw he was hanging on by this time. It wasn't long when Sammy flouted his own promise and was duly evicted. He packed his few belongings. And the ever-popular Sammy Young left town as quietly as the day he arrived some years ago. Why this secret departure? Because

> After he had spent everything, there was a severe famine in that whole country, and he began to be in need. So he went and hired himself out to a citizen of that country, who sent him to his fields to feed pigs. He longed to fill his stomach with the pods that the pigs were eating, but no one gave him anything. (Luke 15:14-16)

Yes, this was his new estate, wanting to feed on pig's pod but could not get any. And Sammy, who took the city and its environs by storm and carried them on his shoulders, had now been reduced to a pauper. Gaping holes under his two remaining footwears were staring at him. His faded dresses made him a laughing stock in the eyes of the small community where he sought refuge. Life clearly announced its starkest realities, and Sammy was forced to embrace them the hard way.

One day, Sammy sat quietly and brooded over events of the past years. He took stock of his life for the first time and the harsh decision he took when he failed to heed to those wise parental counselling. Suffering from malnutrition, tears then rolled down those cheeks pitifully. He longed to go back home. Every fiber of his being yearned and cried to see his folks. Sammy was at a crossroad. But the magnitude of his resistance to all the pieces of advice that were given him and the consequences of his departure, which he undeniably knew would come upon his family, prevented him from settling on such an idea. Though Sammy was lost to the world at this moment, shame and pride wouldn't permit him to give up hope. He believed he could change the dynamics, so he kept struggling to make ends meet.

Yet, no matter how hard he tried, his efforts were not enough to cheat his failures. The toss and turns, culminating in continuous sleepless nights, accompanied by lack of any proper feeding, began to take a toll on his health. That youthful skin with which Sammy left home was wrinkling, causing him to look older than his real age. With all these anecdotes playing before his eyes, he seemed not persuaded to return home. Though at this juncture, there were all indications his young life was ebbing away, he stubbornly would not accept those facts. He was in total denial of these facts. The folks acquainted with him knew something was wrong, and that it wouldn't be long when his life would come tumbling down. Even when these acquaintances stepped in to let him know they were aware, he wouldn't still bulge. He would have exhausted his cache of endurance before he surrendered his ego to reality. Then one day,

> When he came to his senses, he said, 'How many of my father's hired servants have food to spare, and here I am starving to death! I will set out and go back to my father and say

to him: Father, I have sinned against heaven and against you. I am no longer worthy to be called your son; make me like one of your hired servants.' (Luke 15:17-19)

So, a few days after he took this decision - a decision that would redefine his wretched life from then onwards - he mustered courage to step out of that small room for the journey that will take him back home. Sammy looked left and then right, as if he'd regretted this wise and defining decision to go home. No! Not at all. It was the flashback of his days in the big cities - the hot spots and the brothels - that had flooded his mind. These cities welcomed him. They opened their arms wide enough and embraced him. But at the same time brought out and put on display the consequences of his decision. He was bidding this faraway country goodbye, never knowing when he would come back again. He was afraid and heartbroken. Not only for the wasted time and talent, but also for the kind of reception awaiting him on the other side of the journey. Then Sammy took a step, then two, three and before long, this country which received and accommodated him for the past few years, was left behind in a distance and in memory. He was gone, and maybe, gone forever.

Sammy was heading home. His appearance looked shabby and out of place. The clothes on his back told better stories than words could have articulated; tattered and stitched together just to hide his nakedness. He was wretchedly dressed and his hair, unkempt. The whole outward look was repulsive. The son of a widely-known rich man who lacked nothing, was coming home a pale shadow of himself. The realities of life taught him lessons he couldn't have learned through words. There are some truths mere words are not enough to drive them home, but experience. He was a student of that experience and he learned the lessons. How?

Sammy, once a proud and arrogant young man full of himself, was humbled and hammered into respect and love. The world was not at all what he thought he knew while in his father's home. There was, and there is, more to it than could meet the eye. The conditions he encountered and endured when he lost all, helped to shape his worldview: that pride and arrogance don't pay. Every hour, as he passed by homes and hamlets, drew him closer to the family and folks he left behind some years back.

As he walked home, leaving the hills and valleys at the rear, Sammy recalled the days when as a young lad he would go after the animals for no apparent reason. He recalled the voice of his dear mother calling him to stop so he wouldn't fall and hurt himself. He remembered the elder sisters cuddling him and feeling the warmth of their love. That pole with containers at each end the elder brother used to draw water from the stream. He remembered his only brother's attempts to prevent him from following him to the stream. How their mother would come and convince the brother, who would then reluctantly agree to allow him a chance. All these moments played on his mind as he lifted each heavy foot to make a step. But with all these joyous moments flashing back in memory as if they happened just a couple of days ago, he still entertained some fears. Fear of rejection. Fear of refusal. Fear of marginalization. However, he had a bargaining chip and he rehearsed it: "…Father, I have sinned against heaven and against you. I am no longer worthy to be called your son; make me like one of your hired servants." (Luke 15: 18-19)

Would the family embrace him despite all he took them through? The shame, the embarrassment, the ridicule. The insinuations. The finger pointing. Finally, the realization dawned on him that this attitude of his denigrated the name and the fame his family claimed for itself over the years. He thought over and over all these. And the more he did, the more he got confused, agitated and discouraged to return home. Yet there was this inner voice urging him on never to give up. So, slowly Sammy pushed himself towards home. The sun was setting to announce the day was coming to an end. The townsfolk were hurrying up to draw water from the stream before darkness would finally arrive. It was at this moment Sammy got within the periphery of their small town. Some folks passed by him. He could not be recognized, he'd drastically changed. No one was able to make him out. And he never made any attempt to expose himself. Shame and self-pity would not even permit him.

Standing at the gate, as the sun shyly hid behind the mountains, was one of the servants. This servant had been with the family before Sammy was born. Therefore, he knew the young man very well. His eyes played tricks on him when he saw the person drawing nearer. He never suspected seeing him again so, he brushed the whole idea out. He took Sammy for someone else. But the more he attempted to ignore the scene playing before his eyes, the closer he drew. Then much to his surprise, Sammy called him. Immediately, this senior servant turned. And in a shock that would defy description, he raised a loud cry while running toward him. Sammy's father was coming from running an errand.

> …But while he was still a long way off, his father saw him and was filled with compassion for him; he ran to his son, threw his arms around him and kissed him. "The son said to him, 'Father, I have sinned against heaven and against you. I am no longer worthy to be called your son.' (Luke 15: 20, 21)

The news of Sammy returning home spread far and wide. Almost the whole townsfolks trooped in to witness the unfolding event. In his son's honor, the father held a feast to celebrate Sammy's safe comeback.

FOOD FOR THOUGHT

- What would have happened if Sammy had come for more money to return to his wild living?

- What would have happened if Sammy threw his weight around as he demanded the money?
- What would have happened if Sammy had been disrespectful, and even threatened his father?

Chapter 4
MY CHARGE
Philemon and Onesimus

"So if you consider me a partner, welcome him as you would welcome me. If he has done you any wrong or owes you anything, charge it to me. I, Paul, am writing this with my own hand. I will pay it back - not to mention that you owe me your very self." (Philemon 1:17-19).

"Apology is the foundation upon which the building of forgiveness solidly stands. The stronger the foundation of apology, the stronger the building of forgiveness." (Author)

Onesimus listened to him with rapt attention. With his hands clasped, resting those long arms on his thighs and legs crossed, he kept his eyes fixated on Paul. He didn't blink for once, neither did he move any part of his body. He sat very quietly throughout the delivery as unimagined tears pooled in his hidden eyes. Onesimus had never heard words having such effect on him as these before. He could easily testify to the piercing power of those words should it be required of him. The words penetrated his hardened heart. He was intrigued and in dilemma. He sat across from Paul that beautiful and cloudless-sky afternoon in his small prison cell. The Apostle, a master at his craft, took the narrative from the beginning in the garden of Eden. He said, "God created the heaven and earth. He went on to provide everything man would need in the garden before creating him. There was this one tree man was asked not to touch, let alone eat but man flouted this directive. There and then, sin entered the scene, creating a chasm between God and man. Therefore, the characteristics of God, which man inherited from Him when God breathed His breath into man, were distorted. Man was then alienated from God."

Continuing, he said, "Ever since, man's attempt to reconcile with his Maker couldn't materialize. Generation after generation, man became viciously desperate and restless; desperately searching for that reconciliation every and anywhere. Man looked for God in rivers, trees and stones, bowing down to graven images to satisfy that void. Yet it did not meet that need. God felt pity for man, then decided to make a move. So, God in His infinite wisdom and unmeasurable love, sent His Son Jesus to die to bridge that gap. Jesus made that powerful announcement of the essence of His coming and man's responsibility through these words:

> For God so loved the world that he gave his one and only Son, that whoever believes in him shall not perish but have eternal life. For God did not send his Son into the world to condemn the world, but to save the world through him. Whoever believes in him is not condemned, but whoever does not believe stands condemned already because they have not believed in the name of God's one and only Son. (John 3:16-18)

These words bore the whole truth, so "When the people heard this, they were cut to the heart and said to Peter and the other apostles, "Brothers, what shall we do?" (Acts 2:3) Then Paul paused and took another breath.

Paul was under house arrest this time. Yet, visitors were permitted to see him. For that reason, many folks had access to him and his message. Jews, and non-Jews alike, trooped to his place of confinement to hear him speak about this new religion and its teachings. He made persuasive arguments, winning most of them to his side. Paul encouraged his hearers to spread this good news to anyone who would be willing to hear. Through this evangelism, one of Paul's disciples came across Onesimus. Onesimus related his predicament to him. This disciple in turn spoke about him to the Apostle. This runaway slave, having come from the same city as Philemon, encouraged the Apostle to get interested in him.

Over time, Paul invited him to his place. When he finished hearing the incident that brought Onesimus to Rome, the Apostle decided to minister to him. Within a period of time, spanning for about a year, Onesimus began to experience change in his perceptions about life. On that fateful morning as he sat from the man of God, with accumulated tears dripping down his cheeks, he remorsefully asked Paul what he would want him do. As this interaction was taking place, folks were gathering to seek audience with the apostle. The Apostle dismissed him and scheduled the following day for continuation. Slowly, Onesimus lifted his body up and left with the promise to come back again as they agreed. And he did leave.

Hypothetical Offence Committed*

Onesimus was born to poor peasant parents. They were farmers, barely making ends meet. They scratched, they scrubbed, and they scrapped anything that would enable them put food on the table. On the economic ladder, the parents were at the lowest, so raising their children had been difficult all along. He was the oldest child among the five the parents gave birth to. Young Onesimus observed and endured all the difficulties they, as a family, experienced. Therefore, right from the onset, there was every indication Onesimus would be sold into slavery to help alleviate the burden of taking care of the younger ones. The only obstacle on the parent's way was his age. He was too young to be given away. They would have to wait until he was matured enough to attract responsible amount from any willing buyer.

Sturdily, Onesimus was growing to be a young man, full of valor and vigor. Bold and courageous, he attracted attention from folks, both young and old. He exuded joy and was delightful to watch. Onesimus could have easily been any woman's dream husband but for poverty. Yes, poverty blurred who he truly was. In fact, no one recognized him.

Onesimus sat quietly that morning. There was nothing special to do. No one from the community was permitted to go farming or fishing that designated day of the week. It was against the laws of the land. Anyone who flouted these laws were dealt with accordingly. Then the man, whom he saw twice the previous week in their house, greeted him. Though he politely responded with his usual youthful smile, he'd some reservations. And it wouldn't take long when those suspicions would have been confirmed. Negotiations towards his purchase had been finalized. Onesimus was leaving with the stranger. He was going to start a new life in a new home, not as a free man, but a slave. It never dawned on him that this morning would be the last with his folks. In fact, such transactions were common in their small community.

He heard and saw some of their community members who were sold the previous years. It was therefore not so much more a bother for Onesimus to be sold than for the new place. He heard despicable stories told about slavery, so he got worried about the new environment. He thought of the folks he was going to work with. It weighed heavily on him. How they were going to treat him bothered him and was visible. He did not know what was awaiting him on the other side. But he must go, and he went. When all was done, Onesimus hugged his friends and family, then he cleaned those few tears dripping down his cheeks. Amidst pain and sorrow, finally, he left with the stranger. He waved as they walked away. His future was unknown, and there was no way he would return home any time soon, if there was any way at all.

Onesimus was so tired when they arrived at their destination. He had never made a journey so long like this before. It therefore took a heavy toll on him. He felt pain all over his body especially the feet. As he sat down quietly waiting for his master, the young man pulled the little items he carried from home close to him. Then he perused the environment. Everything looked different from what he knew back home. The servants were busy at work. The precision with which they attended to their work indicated the presence of discipline. It was a delight to watch. It looked like every act was thoroughly rehearsed. This waned the fears Onesimus harbored all along. He was eager to join the fray. As he watched all that was happening before his very eyes, he was alerted of the master's presence. Within a few seconds, he was called in to meet him. He picked that little sack containing his few belongings and dashed away to meet him.

Philemon was delighted upon seeing the new addition to his team of slaves. The boss immediately directed he should be taken through the list of chores that were to be performed daily. After that brief orientation, he was assigned to the group that took care of the animals. There and then, he decided to live above expectation. So, by dint of hard work, he rose quickly through the ranks to become the head servant of their department. Onesimus gave off the best of his ability and it paid off. He was trustworthy. For this reason, the boss gave him the opportunity to transact businesses on his behalf.

Onesimus could go days without rendering accounts for the trust that was invested in him. He was exposed to money now and had the ears of his master. It was known all over their estate he carried money from transactions on the master's behalf. And it was this act of faithfulness that cost him dearly, resulting in his flee to Rome. Onesimus was attacked as he returned from a business transaction. It was rumored one of the slaves conspired with the thugs to perpetrate such a crime against him. He was scared to death as he did not know what was awaiting him. Instead of going home to face whatever consequences there might be, he fled to Rome. This decision created the impression that he feigned his identity.

Apology Rendered

A few years had passed now when the Apostle and Onesimus first met. So much had taken place between them by this time. Unfortunately, their relationship started on rocky grounds as the young man resisted the numerous invitations extended to him. This see-saw relationship was not going anywhere yet, the apostle never gave up hope. But upon persistent persuasion, Onesimus agreed to meet the Apostle. He knew Onesimus would reach his wit's end one day, and he did. And when they finally met for the first time, the Apostle's malnutrition face forced a friendly greeting. However, he never hesitated to bluntly condemn him for his decision to bolt away. This confirmed his worst fears, the reason for which he resisted from the beginning. But as they interacted with each other over a period of time, Onesimus gained confidence that the man of God meant no harm. That the man of God had good intentions for his welfare. This meeting was made possible by those who visited Paul earlier on.

How? When he'd depleted his accumulated resources. When life stared at him with its stark realities and evidences. When there was no one now to turn to as his personal life started to spiral down. When atrocities of life kept piling its onslaught on him. When he reached the inflection of his wretched life in Rome, he gave the whole decision to run away a second thought. It was then Onesimus realized the enormity of the decision to run away from his master Philemon. It was then he began to connect the dots. It was then he regretted and felt remorseful for the move he made that fateful day. That if he had paused to consider the consequences of his actions, the outcome could or would have been different. It was then he came to terms with the truth that it doesn't pay to run away from responsibility. It was then the words he had been hearing from Paul began to mean something for him. It was then his eyes and ears were opened to Paul's submissions all along. Then he cracked. The he caved in. Then he decided to embrace Paul. Onesimus' intentions to run away from his master presented some dire consequences. That his action would demand reciprocation of the same magnitude. Paul knew the danger awaiting him if he should return home. Onesimus knew as well. But the Apostle Paul would seize the opportunity to explain to him why he would want him to go back to the master. Then the Apostle quoted Jesus to buttress his argument why he would not want him to remain in Rome if indeed he had accepted his counsel.

> Therefore, if you are offering your gift at the altar and there remember that your brother or sister has something against you, leave your gift there in front of the altar. First go and be reconciled to them; then come and offer your gift. (Matthew 5:23-24)

The young man sat there quietly, taking in every word falling from Paul's mouth. He sternly focused on him. When the apostle finished, Onesimus took the time to sieve all he said. He analyzed everything. It was extremely difficult for him to accept this bargain. The evidence of his inability to accept this bargain was clearly exposed in his facial expression. Paul cleverly noticed it in his demeanor. Then he suggested to Onesimus he would love to plead on his behalf. He would love to tell the story of the change that occurred in his life. The apostle went on to assure him that he would not go all by himself. And truly Paul did provide a chaperone. He wrote a letter to Philemon that his slave was returning home. He spelled out the transformation the young man experienced. The apostle, in writing, infused wisdom and tact into the message he crafted to this offended master. Paul deftly appealed to his conscience and to his heart. He didn't fail to capture the sensitivity of the issue. For that reason, he trod with trepidation. He chose words which would carry his intentions without any objection, and words that would erase any trace of revenge Philemon would want to unleash. And it touched him tremendously, leaving an indelible mark on his mind. Philemon graciously accepted the content of the letter sent to him. Not only that, but also accepted Onesimus. He opened his doors, once again, to this runaway slave, a fugitive to be precise. Someone who caused him tremendous pain and agony. One who does not deserve a second chance in any way, shape or form. One who should be executed upon first sight yet, was spared his life. It was all about Paul's approach. Anything otherwise would have degenerated into gloom and doom. Let us see how Paul crafted his letter.

(1)   Praised him – vv. 4-7

> I always thank my God as I remember you in my prayers, because I hear about your love for all his holy people and your faith in the Lord Jesus. I pray that your partnership with us in the faith may be effective in deepening your understanding of every good thing we share for the sake of Christ. Your love has given me great joy and encouragement, because you, brother, have refreshed the hearts of the Lord's people.

The Apostle Paul knew that Philemon had all the power to do whatever he would want to Onesimus. And any measures he might have taken would've been in place. But for the change that occurred, it would not be prudent if the master should take such drastic measures. So, Paul wisely intervened. He anticipated tempers would flare up upon seeing Onesimus. On that note, the apostle began his letter by heaping praises on the recipient. He brought out the good qualities Philemon possessed and touted their benefits to the body of Christ. Nothing could have been better than this approach. Remember, Onesimus' running away caused some damage to his master; financial and otherwise. And he must pay for, the punishment which would be so hard. It was for this reason Paul crafted the letter in this manner.

(2) Pleaded with him – vv. 8-11

> Therefore, although in Christ I could be bold and order you to do what you ought to do, yet I prefer to appeal to you on the basis of love. It is as none other than Paul - an old man and now also a prisoner of Christ Jesus - that I appeal to you for my son Onesimus, who became my son while I was in chains. Formerly he was useless to you, but now he has become useful both to you and to me.

Paul possessed the apostolic authority to command Philemon into action. To accept Onesimus without any qualms. His apostolic authority permitted him to order these folks to bow to his orders. There would be nothing wrong if Paul commanded the master to open his home to his slave. It wouldn't have been usurpation or abdication of power from Philemon. But he did not go that route. He did not exercise that mandated authority. Instead, he appealed to him "on the basis of love." He failed to boast of the power he possessed as an apostle. He didn't elevate himself above the man. Instead, he came down to his level and appealed to him to consider his submissions.

(3)   Persuaded him – vv. 12-16

> I am sending him - who is my very heart - back to you. I would have liked to keep him with me so that he could take your place in helping me while I am in chains for the gospel. But I did not want to do anything without your consent, so that any favor you do would not seem forced but would be voluntary. Perhaps the reason he was separated from you for a little while was that you might have him back forever - no longer as a slave, but better than a slave, as a dear brother. He is very dear to me but even dearer to you, both as a fellow man and as a brother in the Lord.

When Paul had finished appealing to Philemon, he presented facts to buttress his argument. Philemon's intentions must change if Paul would want him to take Onesimus back. For that reason, his demand must be persuasive and not forceful, as Philemon was reeling in pain caused by the slave's departure. Without mincing words, he said; *"Perhaps the reason he was separated from you for a little while was that you might have him back forever - no longer as a slave, but better than a slave, as a dear brother..." (Philemon vv. 15, 16).* And he nailed it with this choice of words.

(4) Partnered with him – vv. 17-21

> So if you consider me a partner, welcome him as you would welcome me. If he has done you any wrong or owes you anything, charge it to me. I, Paul, am writing this with my own hand. I will pay it back - not to mention that you owe me your very self. I do wish, brother, that I may have some benefit from you in the Lord; refresh my heart in Christ. Confident of your obedience, I write to you, knowing that you will do even more than I ask.

Paul knew the burden of forgiveness would be too heavy for a friend, most especially with regards to a slave running away. Therefore, he cannot leave all the burden on Philemon's shoulder as he sent Onesimus back. He knew evidently something might have been lost with the slave's desertion. Philemon might have incurred some debt. And to compensate the master, Paul requested to partner with him to resettle the returning man. This time not as a slave but, more than that, as a brother in the Lord. Truthfully, Philemon did not deny Paul his request. And there was a beautiful reunion.

FOOD FOR THOUGHT

- What would have happened if Paul had not praised Philemon?
- What would have happened if Paul had not pleaded with him?
- What would have happened if Paul had not persuaded him?
- What would have happened if Paul had not partnered with him?

Chapter 5
MY THOUGHTS
Manner of Apology

Therefore, if you are offering your gift at the altar and there remember that your brother or sister has something against you, leave your gift there in front of the altar. First go and be reconciled to them; then come and offer your gift. (Matthew 5:23-24)

"Apology is the bridge forgiveness crosses over from the island of resentment to the mainland of reconciliation." (Author)

On a few occasions I had been called upon, as the Superintendent of the Sunday School department and a leader in the church to help settle issues. It is so sobering to be called by someone to help solve a problem. Such invitations were the result of the confidence they had invested in me. I therefore didn't, and will not, take them lightly. And in course of finding solutions to such issues, I found out how apology played vital roles in arriving at genuine and peaceful solutions. It's upon such premises that I want to give a shout out to this important phenomenon that had been neglected in solving conflicts.

Therefore, in the course of writing this book, I conceived an idea to help me make an informed argument in support of the subject in question. An informed argument that will bring the truth out and have a bearing on even the skeptics. And that was to seek others' view on apology. So, I interviewed a few folks who willingly offered their take on it. I selected folks from diverse backgrounds and ages but, with a wealth of life experiences. They were males and females, blacks and whites, Latinos and Asians, young and old, Christians and non-Christians alike. I purposely chose this crop of people so as not to slant the result to a specific class. And though they were characterized by different persuasions in their beliefs, they share a common drive, the desire to live peacefully with their neighbors.

I usually began this way, "I need your view over an issue I am wrestling with." "What is it that you want me to do for you," they always enquired from me. In response, I submitted by saying, "With all things being equal, let's say you were offended by two people. One offence is considered not so serious. A minor infraction to be precise. Whiles the other, so serious that when some folks heard of it they were moved. The not-so-serious offender never made any attempt to apologize." Then I would pause to make sure my massage was properly understood. "On the other hand, the serious offender stretched out a hand of apology to you and as well, sought forgiveness." Once again, I would pause for the same reason. Then finally concluding, I would pose my question thus, "Which of these two would you be able to genuinely forgive?" Folks, shockingly without mincing words, they all came to the same conclusion that the one who came forward to apologize and sought forgiveness would be easily forgiven. "The offence is serious, why will you be able to forgive?" I would ask. The common reason was that the offender coming forward to apologize melts heart and softens any tension. It also shows respect and regard for you as a human being. And that is what makes all the difference. The Teacher couldn't have said it better in support of the subject;

> A gentle answer turns away wrath, but a harsh word stirs up anger. The tongue of the wise adorns knowledge, but the mouth of the fool gushes folly" (Proverbs 15:1, 2).

Apology is the lubricant that lubricates the turning wheels of forgiveness. Apology is the fertile soil from which the seed of forgiveness can easily sprout. And these truths cannot be overstated. Its magnificent presence, when cleverly employed, speeds up the process of trashing misunderstandings in any conflict. It should be one of the most demanding ingredients in a feud. Its absence will cause the expected turning wheels of forgiveness to come to an abrupt halt. The inclusion of apology in settling a rift between rival factions will ameliorate the damaged relationship, and in most cases, will obliterate the standing tensions. If the important role of apology is not adequately stressed to the offender so he/she could properly understand, thereby fully rendering it to the offended, forgiveness would not balance but wobble. Ultimately, full forgiveness will not be realized, which will then result in continued strained relationship. But if apology is genuinely and properly extended, it will unleash nuggets of harmony beyond expectation between the parties involved in the conflict.

In fact, my quest to write and make a case for apology stems from a few conclusions I came to when the message of forgiveness is preached from the pulpit or when the word of God is taught on the subject. Forgiveness and its attending quotes are so much stressed during preaching or teaching that it leaves the offended helpless and hopeless. Meanwhile, there is no mention of apology when forgiveness is being discussed as if Jesus didn't address it in the scriptures. It is profoundly disheartening when the offended is bashed to feel guilty for his/her inability to forgive. The offended is turned into the 'offender' and thereby, pushed to act fast in order not to incur the wrath of God. Then, immediately, it is followed by their popular Jesus' quote,

> For if you forgive other people when they sin against you, your heavenly Father will also forgive you. But if you do not forgive others their sins, your Father will not forgive your sins. (Matthew 6:14, 15)

And the victim reeling in pain becomes a pawn in the hands of those who think the offended shouldn't complain irrespective of the magnitude of the pain. Often, the offender is left off the hook. It hurts so much when the offended is caught in this kind of web. For this reason, I decided to use what Jesus said to educate folks on the fundamental importance of apology and its role in amicable solution to issues. The four feuds I discussed on the previous pages, will be the examples from which we will see how apology contributed to bringing about amicable settlement. Though the word - apology - is not exquisitely used in the texts, yet there are traces of it in the narratives. It was expressed through the words and attitudes of the offenders. And they did it so well to bring peaceful solutions to the difficult problems they started.

Jacob's Manner of Apology

It had been twenty years the last time Jacob and Esau saw each other. And over this period, a lot happened in their various lives. Jacob was returning home to friends and family. Folks he'd not seen all this while. But with all the joy accompanying his return, there was something weighing Jacob down; the effects of the deceptions he perpetrated against his brother.

He wanted to mend fences with him, but for the enormity of his behavior. He was aware of the bitterness Esau expressed that fateful day. It was too real to be denied. Very visible in his eyes and very delible on his mind. There was no way he could break through Esau's heart if he failed to express any remorse and thereby apologize for the pains he took him through. He must act, and he acted wisely. Then

> Jacob sent messengers ahead of him to his brother Esau in the land of Seir, the country of Edom. He instructed them: "This is what you are to say to <u>my lord</u> Esau: 'Your servant Jacob says, I have been staying with Laban and have remained there till now. I have cattle and donkeys, sheep and goats, male and female servants. Now I am sending this message to <u>my lord</u>, that I may find_favor in your eyes'" (Genesis 32: 3-5).

The messengers brought back response from his brother and the corresponding action he was taking. They announced Esau was coming to meet him with a battalion of four hundred men. The report got Jacob gripped with tremendous fear. Why? Because of the atrocious sins he committed against his brother, which hanged on his neck like an albatross all this while. He epitomized what the Teacher said, "The wicked flee though no one pursues, but the righteous are as bold as a lion." (Proverbs 28:1) So, he said, "Save me, I pray, from the hand of my brother Esau, for I am afraid he will come and attack me, and also the mothers with their children." (Genesis 32: 11)

But then Jacob's actions thus far could not suffice his intentions, so he went further in seeking peace with Esau. To pacify him, he selected herds of cattle, goats and sheep and sent them ahead. The intention was to soften his heart before they could come face to face with each other. In other words, Jacob was announcing to his brother how sorry he was for what he did to him some years back. With these items, he showed how remorseful he was for the crimes he committed. He sent his messengers ahead, once again, to Esau with these instructions,

> …"When my brother Esau meets you and asks, 'Who do you belong to, and where are you going, and who owns all these animals in front of you?' then you are to say, 'They belong to <u>your servant</u> Jacob. They are a gift sent to <u>my lord</u> Esau, and he is coming behind us.'" He also instructed the second, the third

and all the others who followed the herds: "You are to say the same thing to Esau when you meet him. And be sure to say, 'Your servant Jacob is coming behind us.'" For he thought, "I will pacify him with these gifts I am sending on ahead; later, when I see him, perhaps he will receive me." So Jacob's gifts went on ahead of him, but he himself spent the night in the camp (Genesis 32:17-21)

When Jacob had dispatched his messengers, he paused to reflect upon those painful events he was involved in with his brother. He shook his head in regret, and thought if he could go back in time, he would have acted differently. He thought every move and every gesture Esau made was to send sign of consequences. He could recollect now, just as he saw then, the deep anger on Esau's face. Jacob became tensed and heavy. So, slowly he walked behind the servants at a distance gripped with fears beyond description (Genesis 32:7-12).

Many questions flooded his mind as to what Esau's reaction would be when they finally meet. There was no answer he could settle on to give him some hope. Jacob's perceived answers could not suffice his anxiety and curiosity. There was no way he could escape meeting his brother. Jacob would have to meet him. It had been holding him down. This issue must come to an end, there must be reconciliation. He was at fault and the onus rested on him to make amends. He was afraid, scared to the bones. But he walked a step at a time until finally he saw Esau. Then, "He himself went on ahead and bowed down to the ground seven times as he approached his brother" (Genesis 33:3) What was Esau's response when Jacob acted this way?

> But Esau ran to meet Jacob and embraced him; he threw his arms around his neck and kissed him. And they wept. Then Esau looked up and saw the women and children. "Who are these with you?" he asked Jacob answered, "They are the children God has graciously given your servant" (Genesis 33:4, 5).

How could Esau so easily overcome all the wicked and evil perpetrated against him by his younger brother? How could he gather enough courage to embrace Jacob in his arms and kiss him as if nothing happened between them? Simple. It was Jacob's remorse - accepting responsibility for all the offence he committed against his brother - and thereby rendering his apology, that speeded up the process. Another contributing factor was how he addressed Esau: 'your servant' and 'my lord.' It was this kind of attitude Jacob displayed that convinced his brother that the man coming to meet him had a change of mind and heart. That there had been a transformation in his life. He expressed that by the amount of wealth he gathered and sent ahead of him to his brother. Putting all these gestures and attitude together, it wasn't hard for Esau to read meaning into his brother's message.

David's Manner of Apology

The prophet Nathan had just indicted king David. The crimes committed by impregnating Bathsheba, plotting to kill Uriah and taking her as his wife were too real to be ignored. David knew that. For that matter, he made every effort to cover up but never knew the whole scheme was in God's plain sight. But God revealed it to the prophet and commanded him to confront the king. Nathan did not hesitate a bit, never flinched but made the move to the palace. The prophet then enumerated God would have done more for David if what He did was not sufficient enough for him (2 Samuel 12:7, 8).

(a)   anointed you king over Israel (v. 7),

(b)   delivered you from the hand of Saul (v. 7).

(c)   gave your master's house to you (v. 8),

(d)   your master's wives into your arms (v. 8).

(e)   gave you all Israel and Judah (v. 8).

(f)   had this been too little, would have given you even more (v. 8).

The man of God queried the king. I can imagine God's temper flaring and fluctuating while He spoke through the prophet. How hurtful He was when David ridiculed His name. It beat the prophet's imagination for David to have orchestrated such plot and execute it. "A man after God's own heart?" he might have thought. So, he went further to ask David,

> Why did you despise the word of the Lord by doing what is evil in his eyes? You struck down Uriah the Hittite with the sword and took his wife to be your own. You killed him with the sword of the Ammonites. Now, therefore, the sword will never depart from your house, because you despised me and took the wife of Uriah the Hittite to be your own. (2 Samuel 12:9, 10)

The tone of God's submissions and the prophet's queries in the verses above denoted the magnitude of David's sins. Directly opposite God's nature. The king stood there drenched in disgrace and dishonor, and shrinked to shame and shock. But with courage and his usual humility, interwoven with remorse and regret, David accepted responsibility for all that transpired leading to the death of Uriah and to the taking of Bathsheba. "Then David said to Nathan, "I have sinned against the Lord..."" (2 Samuel 12;13). David let out these words showing his displeasure, indicating a total surrender and taking full responsibility. In other words, "I am sorry for all that I did, God. I am sorry for defying your command, Lord. As the leader of your people, it's incumbent upon me to lead by example." Then this powerful king, caught red-handed in his plot, decidedly knelt in the presence of his subjects and in a loud cry, prayed, appealing to God with these words:

> Have mercy on me, O God, according to your unfailing love; according to your great compassion blot out my transgressions. Wash away all my iniquity and cleanse me from my sin. For I know my transgressions, and my sin

is always before me. Against you, you only, have I sinned and done what is evil in your sight; so you are right in your verdict and justified when you judge. Surely I was sinful at birth, sinful from the time my mother conceived me. Yet you desired faithfulness even in the womb; you taught me wisdom in that secret place.

Cleanse me with hyssop, and I will be clean; wash me, and I will be whiter than snow. Let me hear joy and gladness; let the bones you have crushed rejoice. Hide your face from my sins and blot out all my iniquity. Create in me a pure heart, O God, and renew a steadfast spirit within me. Do not cast me from your presence or take your Holy Spirit from me. Restore to me the joy of your salvation and grant me a willing spirit, to sustain me. Then I will teach transgressors your ways, so that sinners will turn back to you.

Deliver me from the guilt of bloodshed, O God, you who are God my Savior, and my tongue will sing of your righteousness. Open my lips, Lord, and my mouth will declare your praise. You do not delight in sacrifice, or I would bring it; you do not take pleasure in burnt offerings. My sacrifice, O God, is b a broken spirit; a broken and contrite heart you, God, will not despise. May it please you to prosper Zion, to build up the walls of Jerusalem. Then you will delight in the sacrifices of the righteous, in burnt offerings offered whole; then bulls will be offered on your altar. (Psalm 51:1-19)

Though his crimes were very heinous and devastating, David was genuine as it would have been expected of him. His message resonated with God, who then softened His stance against him. In response to David's surrender, "…Nathan replied, "The Lord has taken away your sin. You are not going to die" (2 Samuel 12:13). "How could that had been so simple?" Apology, expressed by David through those words, 'I have sinned against the Lord,' is the summary of it all.

The Prodigal Son's Manner of Apology

Sammy had just entered that small cubicle he occupied as the latest tenant. Then at the center of the room, he paused to check the empty bag he carried. It was still empty. He did this, as if magically something might have dropped into it from somewhere. Like the previous days' outings, nothing had successfully come out of this one too. Life was now unbearable for him. Sammy's attempt to put pieces together were not yielding any fruit. Nothing was coming from his effort. He'd regretted his refusal to see the wisdom gleaned from years of experience by those white-haired men and women who spoke with him. He wished they could be talking to him now, but it was too late. At this juncture the pieces of advice given him by the all these grown-ups, whose help the parents solicited to persuade him began to resonate with reality. Some lessons in life are not learned through mere words, but experience. Sammy sufficed such example. Frustration had set in and seemed to have won the part of him. "What shall I do; what shall I do now?" he asked no one in particular. Quietly, he sat at the edge of his noise-making wooden bed to begin his round of thinking. Then he recalled the site of the pig farm they passed by many times in those heydays. There and then, he decided to check out if he would be hired to work.

The sun had not yet announced its presence across the sky when Sammy stood at the gate of the pen.

There was no way he could have stayed away from this opportunity. Excessive stench pervaded the whole atmosphere. It was so strong that even the poorest of the poor wouldn't accept to work there. But Sammy was in a fix, a position he alone understood. He knocked on that small wooden panel serving as a door to draw attention to his presence. The farmer was surprised looking at the time, yet he responded. When he had known Sammy's reason, he asked the young man to come back after sunrise. Gathering confidence from the farmer's tone, he did just that and he was hired. He began working for the pig farmer with all the strength he had. Slowly, days had ran into weeks. Sammy intensively looked at the condition under which he labored to make ends meet. Even the request to feed on the pig food, since the money he received as salary was not enough to meet his demands. Then uncontrollable tears flooded his eyes, and he felt pity for himself. So,

> When he came to his senses, he said, 'How many of my father's hired servants have food to spare, and here I am starving to death! I will set out and go back to my father and say to him: <u>Father, I have sinned against heaven</u>

and against you. I am no longer worthy to be called your son; make me like one of your hired servants.' So he got up and went to his father... (Luke 15:17-20)

What a surrender for an offence committed? What an acceptance of responsibility for a poor decision? What a move to mend fences with those affected, especially the father? What a display of remorse and regret for an infraction that shouldn't have taken place? These touching words dripping from the lips of his prodigal son pierced and penetrated his heart. His son's demeanor depicted all that needed to be known. And the father knew his son learned his lesson. Without any hesitation, he embraced his lost son, and immediately called for celebration. With all that he might have taken the family through: financial or otherwise, he was easily accepted. Why? It was all loaded in the words spoken to his father.

Paul's Manner of Apology on Onesimus' Behalf

Onesimus' thought of going back to his master had taken a toll on him so far. He thought of the consequences awaiting him should he arrive. He witnessed the punishment meted out to those who ran away before and were captured. Onesimus knew how severe those punishments were. He saw it personally, a firsthand witness. A fellow slave who suffered the consequences of failed attempt to bolt away. To deter other slaves from indulging in such practices, this slave was subjected to a severe maltreatment. A flashback of the event that led to his fleeing flooded his mind. All these events played vividly as he recollected each of them. Onesimus contemplated the whole idea over and over yet, he could convince himself to opt out of it.

And apart from the financial loses, Philemon suffered disgrace and humiliation among his contemporaries. He never anticipated Onesimus running away. Philemon was greatly shocked. He was the least to take such decision. Contemplating, these events conspired against the decision he was supposed to take. It was tough going back, but he must go to reflect his new nature in the Lord. Paul was there to help him make the transition; fugitive to a friend. And he did it profoundly with the content of the letter he wrote on his behalf. He did it with these four points:

- *Praise him,*
- *Pleaded with him,*

- *Persuaded him,*
- *Partnered with him.*

When Philemon had finished reading the letter, he sat quiet for a moment. He was moved beyond expectation. Then he turned towards the runaway slave and embraced him. He squeezed him and planted kisses on both cheeks. This gesture marked a new beginning in their relationship. A useless slave had become a useful friend. Years of resentment were wiped away by the content of a well-crafted letter. What would have happened if Paul chose a different route by commanding Philemon to take Onesimus back without showing any respect? Tried to impose his apostolic authority on his friend instead? Forgiveness is sometimes hard to come forth because of the way an issue is approached. If the offenders would be quickly made aware of the consequences of their behavior, and therefore should apologize, it would encourage them to accept the responsibility. I believe deep down in my heart that if the offenders in the examples above had acted differently, these feuds would have continued and peace would have eluded them.

*The bible did not categorically state the crime he committed before Onesimus ran away. For the sake of presentable narrative, hypothetically I created a scenario.

CONCLUSION

A gentle answer turns away wrath, but a harsh word stirs up anger. The tongue of the wise adorns knowledge, but the mouth of the fool gushes folly. (Proverbs 15:1, 2)

"Forgiveness cannot stand the test of time if apology is not first given the serious consideration it deserves." (Author)

The fundamental reason I am sincerely convinced, apology is scarce in our Christian narratives is because it's not directly mentioned in the Bible. In that sense, ministers of the gospel shy away from it, thereby elevating the messages of forgiveness higher. Forgiveness had so much frequented the pulpit that, apology seems to lack any relevance. Apology had been relegated to the backburner. Therefore, it never received the needed attention and recognition it deserves. It is in this light that I deemed it a great honor done me by the Holy Spirit to see this missing link and help it fixed. That it must be brought to the fore so that its importance is loudly proclaimed. And to achieve this goal, we will consider what the Bible says in Jesus' own words on the subject. First,

> Therefore, if you are offering your gift at the altar and there remember that your brother or sister has something against you, leave your gift there in front of the altar. First go and be reconciled to them; then come and offer your gift. (Matthew 5:23-24)

It was on the mountain when that large crowd followed Him that Jesus made this statement. He took the opportunity to teach them some truths regarding successful human relationships. So, at this juncture, Jesus fruitfully addressed this problem of apology. When you get to the bowl to put in your offering, then you remember you offended your neighbor, thereby holding an offence against you, leave your offering at the altar and be reconciled to him first. Jesus unapologetically said it this way,

*"...**First go and be reconciled to them;...**"* (Matthew 5:24). What does it constitute in the reconciliation process? According to the authors in their book, *"The Five Languages of Apology,"* they said, this process involves the following:

(a)   express regret (I am sorry),

(b)   accepting responsibility (I was wrong),

(c)   making restitution (What can I do to make it right?),

(d)   genuinely repenting (I'll try not to do that again), and

(e)   requesting forgiveness (Will you forgive me?)

(Chapman G. and Thomas J., 2006).

This is what is just required of the offender. After this process then, one can go and put the offering in the bowl. Are there any consequences regarding refusal to apologize? Will the offender be spared of any consequences if after all evidences are laid bare but refuses to accept responsibility and apologize? Yes! How did Jesus approach that? In the ensuing verse, He said it thus;

> Settle matters quickly with your adversary **[the offended]** who is taking you **[offender]** to court. Do it while you are still together on the way, or your adversary **[offended]** may hand you **[offender]** over to the judge, and the judge may hand you **[offender]** over to the officer, and you **[offender]** may be thrown into prison. (Matthew 5:25).

In other words, if the offended takes his/her case to the court of the judge, for the offender's refusal to go through the process of reconciliation, he/she will be handed over to be punished by being sent to prison. So, there are consequences if one refuses to apologize, just as one's refusal to forgive attracts same.

The second point made on apology is in this verse.

> "If your brother or sister sins, go and point out their fault, just between the two of you. **If they listen to you**, you have won them over. But **if they will not listen,** take one or two others along, so that 'every matter may be established by the testimony of two or three witnesses.' If **they still refuse to listen,** tell it to the church; and **if they refuse to listen**

even to the church, treat them as you would a pagan or a tax collector. (Matthew 18:15-17).

In examining these verses, the basic question I ask is, 'Why would Jesus command the offended to keep on seeking a listening ear from the offender until the issue is settled?' The whole reason Jesus wants the offended to continue pursuing the offender is just for the offender to accept responsibility and apologize to pave way for forgiveness. Forgiveness will not be as effective as we would want it to be if apology does not precede it. Like the explanation from the previous texts, any refusal to accept responsibility and thereby apologize, would attract consequences that will squarely fall on the offender's shoulders. And in these texts, the offender will be treated **"as you would a pagan or a tax collector."**

Thirdly, Jesus emphasize the importance of apology when He addressed the Pharisees, the Apostles and the other disciples who listened to Him;

> …"If your brother or sister sins against you, rebuke them; and if they **repent, forgive them.** Even if they sin against you seven times in a day and seven times come back to

you saying **'I repent,'** you must forgive them" (Luke 17:3,4).

As human as we are, we will not escape the squabbles that are associated with our relationships. There is no way we will be able to avoid them. They will come and, come in different ways and forms. At the work place, our homes, churches and anywhere human beings are gathered. These petty issues and more serious ones will continue to plague man until the last exits this earth. So, apology is crucial. Apology is imperative in our human discourse, most especially our time now where little issues have become breeding grounds for seeds of discord and disfunction. For example, the sharp disagreement between Paul and Barnabas, which escalated to a hot argument and culminated in parting ways with each other (Acts 15:36-40). Even men with this high spiritual caliber had differences. Why not us: you and me? We would be able to curb these tensions if we would realize we're humans and therefore not perfect. That we will hurt each other through our actions and words. We might even ill-treat others without being aware of it. These are hard facts that cannot be denied. If we could quickly accept responsibility when we are prompted for the infraction we might cause the other party, little moles will not morph to huge mountains we cannot contain. Even God, whose love is so big enough to contain any sin, would want man to confess his sins before he is forgiven. In other words, man is required to own up to his infractions and apologize. Apostle John couldn't have said it better when he perfectly made the argument that,

> If we claim to be without sin, we deceive ourselves and the truth is not in us. If we **confess our sins,** he is faithful and just and will forgive us our sins and purify us from all unrighteousness. (1 John 1:8, 9)

In the stories cited in the pages of this book, from which I highlighted the importance of apology, Esau was able to forgive Jacob, God forgave David, the prodigal son's father was able to forgive him, and Philemon accepted the Apostle Paul's plea on Onesimus' behalf for one reason. The offenders did not throw their weights around but humbly appealed to the conscience of the offended through their attitudes and words. Simply put, they expressed regret for their actions, accepted responsibility, requested for forgiveness and attempted to make restitutions. On a whole, apology they rendered to their victims was the power that changed hearts and restored lost relationships.

REFERENCE

Chapman, G. & Thomas, J. (2006), *The Five Languages of Apology*, Chicago, IL: Northfield Publishing, pp. 20; 136.

Hughes, R. Kent, (1991), *DISCIPLINES of a GODLY MAN*, Wheaton, IL: Crossway Books, p. 25.

Made in United States
Orlando, FL
11 August 2022